Because Digital Writing Matters

Because Digital Writing Matters

IMPROVING STUDENT WRITING IN ONLINE AND MULTIMEDIA ENVIRONMENTS

National Writing Project

with Dànielle Nicole DeVoss,

Elyse Eidman-Aadahl,

and Troy Hicks

JOSSEY-BASS
A Wiley Imprint
www.josseybass.com

Published by Jossey-Bass
A Wiley Imprint
989 Market Street, San Francisco, CA 94103-1741—www.josseybass.com

Jossey-Bass books and products are available through most bookstores. To contact Jossey-Bass directly call our Customer Care Department within the U.S. at 800-956-7739, outside the U.S. at 317-572-3986, or fax 317-572-4002.

Jossey-Bass also publishes its books in a variety of electronic formats. Some content that appears in print may not be available in electronic books.

Library of Congress Cataloging-in-Publication Data
Because digital writing matters : improving student writing in online and multimedia environments / National Writing Project ; with Dànielle Nicole DeVoss, Elyse Eidman-Aadahl, and Troy Hicks.—1st ed.
   p. cm.
  Includes bibliographical references and index.
  ISBN 978-0-470-40772-1 (pbk.)
  ISBN 978-0-4708-9220-6 (ebk.)
  ISBN 978-0-4708-9221-3 (ebk.)
  ISBN 978-0-4708-9223-7 (ebk.)
  1. English language—Rhetoric—Computer-assisted instruction.   2. English language—Rhetoric—Study and teaching.   3. English language—Composition and exercises—Computer-assisted instruction.   4. English language—Composition and exercises—Study and teaching.   5. Report writing—Computer-assisted instruction.   6. Report writing—Study and teaching.   7. Electronic portfolios in education.   8. Multimedia systems.   I. DeVoss, Dànielle Nicole.   II. Eidman-Aadahl, Elyse.   III. Hicks, Troy.   IV. National Writing Project (U.S.)
  PE1404.B43 2010
  808'.0420785—dc22

2010023119

Printed in the United States of America

FIRST EDITION

PB Printing   10 9 8 7 6 5 4 3 2 1

CONTENTS

PREFACE

Teachers of writing have always had a consuming interest in the tools of writing. Whether it is the search for the perfectly sized journal or the choice of just the right background and style for our blogs, the writer in us knows that tools matter, that tools shape the user as the user shapes the tools. So it is of little surprise that many writing teachers were among the early adopters of new digital tools for writing. From early work with word processing software, HyperCard stacks, and desktop publishing to the participatory affordances of blogs, wikis, and the read/write Web, writing teachers have been wandering the digital frontier for some time.

The National Writing Project (NWP) can trace its work with writing and technology to the early 1990s when groups of teachers, such as the "Net-heads," and early online communities, such as Urbnet and the E-Anthology, laid the foundation for sustained attention to new networked and digital technologies at local Writing Project sites. Over the years these efforts grew, and Writing Project sites named "technology liaisons" to their local leadership teams, applied for minigrants to support their work with technology, attended tech-focused networking events like the NWP's Tech Matters retreats, fostered a national special-focus network to share and support one another, and nurtured local technology teams. NWP sites were considering how best to use these technologies in their teaching and professional development repertoires because of the technologies' profound impacts and the questions raised about the very nature of writing and learning to write.

In 2003, the NWP received federal support to mount a substantial program—the Technology Initiative—to broadly expand opportunities at local Writing Project sites for professional development in technology and the teaching of writing. More than twenty Writing Project sites received support to research and design new approaches to professional development that would engage teachers in creating the kinds of environments where young people would and could learn to be writers, creators, and participants in a digital age. Throughout the initiative, teachers brought to the surface powerful examples of classroom practice that suggested what it might mean to teach writing in a digital age, developed frameworks for professional development for colleagues, and continued to ask themselves hard questions about literacy learning.

In 2007, at a culminating meeting of the initial Technology Initiative, a study team of seventy-three lead teachers and scholars from around the country explored this work together through facilitated discussions of cases of classroom practice presented by teachers in the NWP and the Bread Loaf Teacher Network (BLTN), another early adopter of digital writing as central in the English language arts curriculum. The rationale was straightforward: teachers in these networks had been experimenting long enough with writing in digital environments that collective interrogation of their work was likely to generate some degree of shared knowledge—and important new questions—about emerging classroom practices and the opportunities for student learning that they did or did not create.

In many ways, that conference—and subsequently this book—captured a turning point in the NWP network's thinking about digital writing. The original question of the Technology Initiative—How can we effectively integrate technology into our teaching?—both reflected a commitment to technology's inherent potential to have an impact on the teaching of writing and indicated the degree to which we conceived of technology and writing as separate. But the cases presented in the conference, as well as the conversations they provoked, pointed us to an important shift in emphasis that has emerged in our collective work with technology since 2003, and the title of this book points to that shift. We began to see that the issue was no longer "technology" or "tech integration" per se. The issue was writing itself.

At the close of that conference, participants Dànielle Nicole DeVoss and Troy Hicks suggested that what the NWP needed was a companion to its popular book *Because Writing Matters* that would take up this insight about technology in writing. In a small postconference meeting with Elyse Eidman-Aadahl and Christina Cantrill, the plan for *Because Digital Writing Matters* was created.

In the three years since that initial Technology Initiative conference, the challenges and the opportunities have only become more clear. Writing today is pervasively and generally digital: composed with digital tools; created out of word, image, sound, and motion; circulated in digital environments; and consumed across a wide range of digital platforms. Even when we read and write with paper—as we certainly do now and will continue to do for a long time to come—we bring to that paper a different understanding of what writing is and can be, based on our experiences in the digital world. This evolving understanding of writing, which informs the ideas conveyed in this book, also undergirds our new efforts around digital writing. With the support of the John D. and Catherine T. MacArthur Foundation's Digital Media and Learning Initiative, we now embark on an effort to support an emerging field of practice, that of teaching writing in the twenty-first century.

So with this book we ask the question: Why does digital writing matter? Digital writing matters because we live in a networked world and there's no going back. Because, quite simply, *digital is.*

THE AUTHORS

The National Writing Project (NWP) envisions a future where every person is an accomplished writer, engaged learner, and active participant in a digital, interconnected world. The NWP is a nationwide network of educators working together to improve the teaching of writing in the nation's schools and in other settings. The NWP provides high-quality professional development programs for teachers in a variety of disciplines and at all levels, from early childhood through university. Founded in 1974 at the University of California, Berkeley, the NWP today is a network of more than two hundred university-based sites located in all fifty states, the District of Columbia, Puerto Rico, and the U.S. Virgin Islands. Codirected by faculty from the local university and K–12 schools, each NWP site develops a leadership cadre of teachers through an invitational summer institute, and designs and delivers customized professional development programs for local schools, districts, and higher education institutions. NWP sites serve over 130,000 participants annually, reaching millions of students. For more information, please visit www.nwp.org.

Dànielle Nicole DeVoss is an associate professor and director of the Professional Writing Program at Michigan State University. Her research interests include multimodal composing; computer-technological literacies; K–12 partnerships and connections; and intellectual property issues in digital space. With Dickie Selfe, DeVoss worked to establish the Electronic Communication Across the Curriculum workshop for middle and high school students and teachers. DeVoss's work has most recently appeared in *Computers and Composition; Computers and Composition Online,* and *Kairos: A Journal of Rhetoric, Technology, and Pedagogy.* DeVoss recently coedited (with Heidi McKee) *Digital Writing Research: Technologies, Methodologies, and Ethical Issues* (Hampton Press, 2007), which won the 2007 Computers and Composition Distinguished Book Award. She is currently working on an edited collection with Martine Courant Rife and Shaun Slattery, titled *Copy(write): Intellectual Property in the Composition Classroom.*

Elyse Eidman-Aadahl directs National Programs and Site Development at the National Writing Project at the University of California, Berkeley. She has been a high school English and journalism teacher, an educator professor, and a director of the Maryland Writing Project at Towson University. In her current role, Eidman-Aadahl oversees national learning networks and professional development programs for the National Writing Project, a network of more than two hundred university-based local sites. As a scholar, she has directed numerous action research networks in the United States and abroad that focus on engaging teachers, youth practitioners, and young people in the study of literacy as a sociocultural-material practice. Winner of the Hollis Caswell Award, she has published in a range of journals and coedited *Writing for a Change: Boosting Literacy and Learning Through Social Action* (2006), published by Jossey-Bass.

Troy Hicks is an assistant professor of English at Central Michigan University (CMU) and focuses on the teaching of writing; writing across the curriculum; literacy and technology; and teacher education and professional development. In his research, he collaborates with K–12 teachers and explores how they implement newer literacies in their classrooms. He is director of CMU's Chippewa River Writing Project, a site of the National Writing Project, and he frequently conducts professional development workshops related to writing and technology. Hicks is author of the book *The Digital Writing Workshop* (Heinemann, 2009) and writes the blog Digital Writing, Digital Teaching, which explores issues related to teaching writing with new media for K–12 teachers and teacher educators: hickstro.org/.

INTRODUCTION

Why Digital Writing Matters

> In today's complex, high-technology world, the importance of writing as a fundamental organizing objective of education is no less valid or practical. Writing, properly understood, is thought on paper. Increasingly, in the information age, it is also thought on screen, a richly elaborated, logically connected amalgam of ideas, words, themes, images, and multimedia designs.
>
> —*The Neglected "R"*, 2003, 13

Because Writing Matters: Improving Student Writing in Our Schools (National Writing Project and Carl Nagin, 2006), originally published in 2003, argued for the irreducible importance of writing. In the years since its publication, the basic argument of *Because Writing Matters* remains unchanged. Writing is still an important act and an essential tool for learning and social participation. Skill in writing is still crucial inside and outside of our schools. Writing is still recognized as a socially situated act of great complexity. And writing is still understood to be hard work.

However, in this volume, *Because Digital Writing Matters*, we argue that—despite the short time frame—much *has* changed in the landscape of what it means to "write" and to "be a writer" since 2003. Social networking and collaborative writing technologies have taken hold, if not always in our schools, certainly among our students. Bandwidth has increased in many locations, along with wireless access. Spaces and devices for creating, sharing, and distributing writing have become more robust and more accessible. Not only does writing matter, but *digital* writing matters.

Numerous reports and policy statements document this shift in our thinking about education and writing, including two National Commission on Writing reports: *The Neglected "R": The Need for a Writing Revolution* (2003) and *Writing: A Ticket to Work . . . Or a Ticket Out* (2004). The National Council of Teachers of English, a professional association for teachers of English language arts, has added digital writing to its list of concerns with two reports: *21st Century Literacies* (2007) and *Writing Now* (2008b). And significantly, the framework for the National Assessment of Educational Progress (NAEP) in Writing has determined that its assessment will be conducted in a computer environment. In 2003, *The Neglected "R"* noted four challenges ahead, one of which was the integration of technology into the teaching and learning of writing. In just a few short years—with the advent of what have been variously called "Web 2.0," "read/write Web," and "cloud computing" technologies—we no longer see technology integration as a challenge ahead, but a challenge that we face daily in our classrooms, our hallways, our school districts, and our world.

Although all of the reports above document the changing context for writing and the need for students to harness twenty-first-century information and communication tools for writing, each of these reports also notes one constant: writing matters. And if writing matters, so too do the roles that teachers and schools play in teaching writing and supporting literacy. Young people today have an unprecedented level of access to a wider range of content and connectivity than ever before, yet access does not ensure that reflection and learning take place. Student writers still need thoughtful and well-prepared teachers and mentors. Computers will not replace teachers, nor should they. Teachers of writing have a crucial role in supporting students in understanding the complexities of communicating in a twenty-first-century world.

Because Digital Writing Matters aims to contribute to this larger aim, but from a particular vantage point. Specifically, this book will argue that—as the title suggests—*digital* writing matters. In the past, when we thought of writing, we often imagined a solitary author sitting at a desk, perhaps holding a pencil or pen, scribbling on paper. When we thought of classrooms, we might have imagined a room filled with desks organized into rows all facing a teacher's desk at the front of the space, students sitting, heads bent, writing on notebook paper with pencils. These notions likely feel a bit strange to American students today, many of whom maintain social networking profiles, write regularly (if not daily) via instant and text messages, blog, and perform many of their other daily writing-related tasks at computers. As documented in the Digital Youth Project, a three-year ethnographic look at young people and digital media; young people are engaged in a multipurpose, highly participatory, "always on" relationship with digital media (Ito et al., 2008). School, in contrast, is seriously "unplugged."

Few changes are as important for educators as those that affect the experiences of our students. One notable video that outlines these changes is Colorado educator Karl Fisch's *Did You Know?: Shift Happens* (original version not available), originally created for a professional development session in his school district. Within one year of YouTube publication, the video had been viewed more than four million times. About a year after the original video was published on YouTube, Scott McLeod—of the educational policy and administration faculty at the University of Minnesota— modified the video, enhancing the graphical content and replacing the original music. About six months after that, Fisch and McLeod worked together to create *Did You Know? 2.0* (2007). The collaboratively crafted 2.0 version of the video has been viewed more than ten million times. The video presents some dramatic statistics, for example:

> "Today's 21-year-olds have played 10,000 hours of video games, and they've sent/received 250,000 e-mails or instant messages."
>
> "There were more than 2.7 billion searches performed on Google, 2,700,000,000! . . . this month."
>
> "There are students in China, Australia, Austria, Bangladesh, and the USA who collaborate on projects every day."

Another notable video is Kansas State University anthropologist Michael Wesch's *A Vision of Students Today* (2007), in which he and his students collaboratively document how young people engage with digital media. In a cultural climate in which some are quick to claim that students don't write or read, this video cites examples that show the opposite, such as that 200 students made more than 360 edits to one online document, and that a student who will write 42 pages for her college classes in one semester will also compose over 500 pages of e-mail in that same time frame. In both of these cases—as well as many, many more that are happening in classrooms around the world—students and teachers are documenting the social changes they are experiencing and noting the ways in which technology is influencing how we compose messages for increasingly broader audiences. And in addition to documenting the shift, these products themselves exemplify the shift. Prior to the advent of these new digital tools it would have been impossible to imagine that products made by individual teachers or students and circulated outside of the usual tracks of publishing distribution systems would be able to quickly find such a large, worldwide audience.

The key reason for the shift is the networked computer and related devices. Many current educators will remember the introduction of computerized word processing into the writing process. This technological tool provided significant benefits for writers that teachers quickly integrated into their practices. Word processing and desktop publishing allowed writers to create texts that were much more polished in design and able to integrate image and graphic elements with ease, but it did not fundamentally shift the modes of distribution. Today, however, most computers are connected to the Internet and, increasingly, people can connect via mobile phones as well. These devices have become tools for writing; publishing; distributing; collaborating; interacting; and remixing and mashing together image, word, sound, motion, and more into something that goes far beyond our original vision of what they could do. It is something more properly thought of as a whole new ecology with a wide range of practices. In this book, it is this larger vision of writing to which we refer when we use the term *digital writing.* Digital writing is not simply a matter of learning about and integrating new digital tools into an unchanged repertoire of writing processes, practices, skills, and habits of mind. Digital writing is about the dramatic changes in the ecology of writing and communication and, indeed, what it means to write—to create and compose and share.

As the Writing in Digital Environments (WIDE) Research Collective noted, "Networked computers create a new kind of writing space that changes the writing process and the basic rhetorical dynamic between writers and readers. Computer technologies have changed the processes, products, and contexts for writing in dramatic ways" (2005). Equipping students to write in only one mode—traditionally, black ink on white paper in scripted genres—will not serve students in their higher education experiences or in the workplaces of the future. Equipping students to work across and within contemporary networked spaces, and to write in a range of genres and a diversity of modes to audiences local and widespread, will serve students in their higher education experiences and in the workplaces of the future.

> Teachers of writing are central in the work of reimagining literacy in the digital age—and such reimagining must become central to them. Teachers at all levels and across all subjects will play a vital role for young people in helping them to learn to think critically about new media, to develop an understanding of social and ethical issues involved in all forms of communication, and to recognize the evolving nature of 'authorship,' 'audience' and knowledge itself in an instantly public, global communications environment. Teachers need an opportunity to look beyond the initial change process regarding the introduction of ICT tools and new media to the moment when digital simply is.
>
> —Elyse Eidman-Aadahl,
> "Digital Is . . ." Convening, November 2009.

DEFINING DIGITAL WRITING

So if digital writing is something more than simple text production using a computer and word processing software, what is it? Any review of current publications, policies, or standards projects reveals a broad set of definitions of digital writing, from basic to elaborate. In the blog State of the Art (2005), digital artist Chris Joseph reviewed a range of publications and interviewed a variety of digital writers and multimedia artists about digital writing. Most respondents initially said something along the lines of "Digital writing is hard to define, because technologies change so quickly." But after this initial claim, many interviewees linked their definitions to the affordances offered by new digital tools that make new products and practices possible. For these interviewees, digital writing was

"Any writing that requires a computer to access it." (JodiAnn Stevenson)

"Writing which, at minimum, would be diminished if it were presented in a non-digital format, and at best, which is effectively untranslatable out of the digital format." (Dan Waber)

"Creative writing that uses digital tools/software as an integral part of its conception and delivery." (Catherine Byron)

"Collaborative/participatory writing, hypertext writing, improvisatory 'real time' writing, new media writing (i.e. multimedia authorship), code poetry and programmatic writing, online role playing, journal writing/blogging, international community building, E-learning, game playing . . ." (Tim Wright)

We could, of course, go back even further in terms of humanity's literacy practices, and define digital writing quite broadly, to argue that it is any act that involves writing, inscribing, or scripting using one's digits (that is, fingers or toes). The human species has a long history, then, with digital writing. From the petroglyphs of British Columbia, inscribed onto rock by the Nuxalk people between five and ten thousand years ago, to the richly illuminated manuscripts that have been salvaged from the eighth century, humans have been making meaning on various surfaces using a variety of tools. Angela Haas, a cultural rhetorics scholar and composition teacher, argues that the computer is just one way of encoding information, and reminds us that we have used our digits in texts that range from the "Mesopotamian Cuneiform, to the Egyptian and Mayan hieroglyphs, Chinese logograms, Aztec codices, to American Indian wampum belts, pictographs and petroglyphs" (2008, 28). Indeed, as computers, scanners, digital cameras and camcorders, voice recorders, and mobile phones that can do all of these tasks become ubiquitous, these original acts of inscription are becoming easier to replicate and capture with digital media.

Rather than attempt to cover the long human history of meaning making, however, for the purposes of *Because Digital Writing Matters*, we define digital writing as *compositions created with, and oftentimes for reading or viewing on, a computer or other device that is connected to the Internet.* This in itself is a transformation in the ways in which we write. The bigger transformation is, however, the networked ways in which we can share, distribute, and archive digital compositions using Internet-based technologies. Today's network connectivity allows writers to draw from myriad sources, use a range of media, craft various types of compositions representing a range of tools and genres, and distribute that work almost instantaneously and sometimes globally. Michael Crawford, one of Chris Joseph's interviewees (2005), summed up the new possibilities of digital writing well: "I like to think of it as a totally new place . . . where one can experience freedom of form and from the boundaries now imposed." And for Alison Clifford, "The most positive aspect of digital writing has come from the need to re-think writing and how stories are told. Digital writing requires us to think of multiple possibilities and interpretations of events throughout the narrative and perhaps it encourages a more comprehensive way of thinking about the story as a result."

a transformation

WHAT THE PUBLIC HAS TO SAY ABOUT DIGITAL WRITING

Apart from the experts who have been studying digital writing and, as we might expect, advocating for greater attention to it, what does the public have to say about digital writing and the use of new technologies in writing more generally? Stories in the popular press point to phenomena as diverse as whiz-kid Internet start-ups and cell-phone novels on the one hand, and inflammatory bloggers, Internet predators, and cyberbullying on the other. In the midst of all this change, what do parents think?

A 2008 Pew Internet Research study (Lenhart, Arafeh, Smith, and Macgill, 2008) surveyed teens and parents regarding digital writing. The study found that it is hard to get teens to talk about writing with technology because technology so suffuses their lives that it is often invisible to them and, in turn, they do not consider what they do to be "writing."

Parents, however, were more attentive to the roles that technology plays in writing, and writing well:

- ✓ Parents believe that good writing skills are crucial for future success and point toward an increasing need for good writing skills.
- ✓ Parents, overall, were more likely to argue that students write better with computers because they can revise and edit easily, present ideas clearly, and be creative.
- ✓ Parents were concerned that computers allow for taking shortcuts, not putting effort into writing, using poor spelling and grammar, and writing too fast and carelessly.

A 2007 survey of public opinion on writing in schools (Belden Russonello & Stewart, 2007) that specifically assessed responses to new technologies found that

- ✓ Learning to use a computer at a very young age is a widely endorsed goal—with computer use falling after reading, writing, and math as key skills.
- ✓ Generally, the public believes computers and other new technologies have a more positive than negative impact on teaching students to write well.
- ✓ Better quality of student work on tasks such as research and reports are positive outcomes that most people see from computer use.
- ✓ Americans generally agree that a variety of applications that young people use in their school and social activities—creating slideshow presentations, doing homework on their computers, creating Web pages, writing blogs, and e-mailing friends and family—are contributing positively to their growth as writers.
- ✓ However, instant messaging is seen as harmful to young people's attention spans, and using computers to write is suspected of encouraging carelessness with grammar and spelling.

Figure I.1 provides a snapshot of the value parents place on certain activities, and the concerns they have about specific digital writing practices.

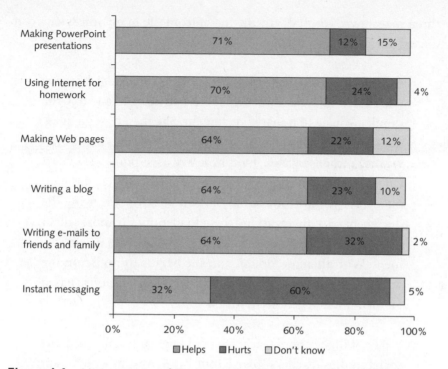

Figure I.1 Various Uses of Computers and Their Impact on Writing
Source: Belden Russonello & Stewart, 2007, 33.

These surveys demonstrate that families are interested in seeing schools take advantage of new digital tools to help students learn and compose. But parents are not interested in students' simply being turned toward technology indiscriminately, and they are sometimes conflicted about whether these tools help or hurt. Not all tools and technologies are perceived equally, and parents expect educators to exercise judgment in pursuing digital writing.

WHAT MIGHT DIGITAL WRITING LOOK LIKE IN THE CLASSROOM?

From the experts we hear that digital writing is both something we *do* using digital tools, and a way of being and working together as we use the tools. From parents we hear that students should use new digital tools to pursue important learning goals. What does this look like in a classroom? Here are three snapshots of digital writing drawn from the many interviews conducted during the process of crafting this book:

An elementary teacher invites her students into a collaborative word processing space where they are able to log in and to write simultaneously to a shared document. She then poses a question about the book they are reading, and students begin typing their responses, anonymously, as well as responses to others. Once everyone has contributed to the document, she pulls it up on a projector in front of the class and begins reviewing the document with them, asking them to identify the most salient responses, which then get copied and pasted into a new document. With this new document, she begins to revise on the screen and teach them how to write a reading response based on their initial reactions to the book.

A pair of high school teachers—one English teacher and one social studies teacher—plan a multiweek unit in which their students will engage in community-based research and represent their work as a digital story or short film at a final exhibition night. <u>Students begin by generating topics and questions</u> *Valuable* <u>that they would like to ask</u> members of their community and posting those ideas to a project wiki, one shared by multiple sections of these two teachers' classes throughout the day. Over the course of the project, students collect artifacts with digital tools such as voice recorders and video cameras, documenting their work on the project wiki. Once the videos are produced, a process that takes nearly two weeks of gathering, organizing, editing, and merging media, students celebrate by inviting the community members they interviewed to the school for the exhibition night. Eventually, many videos are posted on a video-sharing site to allow people from outside the community to see what the students have discovered in their research.

+ then students reflect...

In middle school classrooms across the country, teachers invite their students to compose their thoughts through regular blog postings on a school-hosted social network. As students develop their ideas over the course of many weeks, they also seek other bloggers in the cross-country network with similar interests and make comments on their blog posts, thus participating in peer response and gaining additional ideas for their own research. At the end of the semester, students review their blog posts, find the three that they think best represent their growth as writers over time, and integrate them into a final report on a particular topic, accompanied by a reflection on their writing process.

In each of these vignettes we see many elements of classroom practice and academic learning that would look familiar to teachers and families. But we also see new opportunities for creating, collaborating, communicating, and especially *learning*; and with these new opportunities come new challenges in supporting students to navigate the digital landscape wisely and well.

WHY DIGITAL WRITING MATTERS

Writing instruction appropriate for the world today requires us to consider what new skills and dispositions students might need for the digital age. Henry Jenkins and colleagues at Project New Media Literacies have begun to do just that, suggesting that new media literacies support and demand a highly participatory culture. In *Confronting the Challenges of Participatory Culture: Media Education for the 21st Century* (2006, 4), they note, "Participatory culture shifts the focus of literacy from one of individual expression to community involvement. The new literacies almost all involve social skills developed through collaboration and networking. These skills build on the foundation of traditional literacy, research skills, technical skills, and critical analysis skills taught in the classroom."

The new skills of participatory culture they have identified include the following:

Play: the capacity to experiment with one's surroundings as a form of problem-solving

Performance: the ability to adopt alternative identities for the purpose of improvisation and discovery

Simulation: the ability to interpret and construct dynamic models of real-world processes

Appropriation: the ability to meaningfully sample and remix media content

Multitasking: the ability to scan one's environment and shift focus as needed to salient details

Distributed Cognition: the ability to interact meaningfully with tools that expand mental capacities

Collective Intelligence: the ability to pool knowledge and compare notes with others toward a common goal

Judgment: the ability to evaluate the reliability and credibility of different information sources

Transmedia Navigation: the ability to follow the flow of stories and information across multiple modalities

Networking: the ability to search for, synthesize, and disseminate information

Negotiation: the ability to travel across diverse communities, discerning and respecting multiple perspectives, and grasping and following alternative norms

Visualization: the ability to interpret and create data representations for the purposes of expressing ideas, finding patterns, and identifying trends

The New Media Literacies skills can apply to a wide range of tasks and situations. Similarly, the National Council of Teachers of English (NCTE) suggests in its "NCTE Framework for 21st Century Curriculum and Assessment" (2008a) that teachers frame questions about their curriculum, instruction, and assessment around broad themes to help students

- Develop proficiency with the tools of technology
- Build relationships with others to pose and solve problems collaboratively and cross-culturally
- Design and share information for global communities that have a variety of purposes

- Manage, analyze, and synthesize multiple streams of simultaneously presented information
- Create, critique, analyze, and evaluate multimedia texts
- Attend to the ethical responsibilities required by complex environments

Defining these broad areas of skill and curriculum, though, does not obviate the necessity for attention to specific skills and capacities associated with digital writing. Scholars and teachers like Stuart Selber (2004a, 2004b) and Dànielle DeVoss and Dickie Selfe (2002), who have been pioneers in the field of digital writing, have drawn on their experiences to identify areas of concern for teachers of writing. As writing teachers, they call on their colleagues to develop practices that attend to the wide range of functional, critical, and rhetorical skills that digital writing demands:

- **Functional**
  - Support students' comfort with the seemingly mundane but crucial aspects of digital writing, including file saving, file storage, and file transfer.
  - Help enhance students' familiarity with different application types (for example, word processing, mind mapping, slideshow creation), and with which applications best support which genres.
  - Support students in understanding the anatomy of different digital texts (for example, the coding, scripting, database, or other elements underneath different digital compositions).

- **Critical**
  - Engage students not only in the technical (how-to) aspects of work with digital communication and composition media and technologies but also with the critical skills required to approach those media.
  - Promote the understanding of both writing and technology as complex, socially situated, and political tools through which humans act and make meaning.
  - Encourage students to recognize that composing takes place within, is shaped by, and serves to shape social, educational, and political contexts.

- Encourage students to practice composing, revising, and editing (through and with text, graphics, sound, and still and moving images) using computers and communication technologies to improve their skills as writers.

- **Rhetorical**
  - Address the rhetorical complications and implications of paper-based and digitally mediated texts to enhance the critical dimensions of students' thinking and writing.
  - Encourage students to explore different computer and communication technologies so that they may choose the best technology to facilitate their writing and the rhetorical situation to which they are responding.
  - Recognize that the rhetorical dimensions of the spaces in which students write complicate the rhetorical purposes for which students write. The rhetorical dimensions of the spaces include the arguments embedded within and expressed through the pull-down menus and formatting options of software, for example, and within the dynamics of virtual spaces, where students negotiate e-mail discussion lists, instant messages, Web pages, and other compositions.

Regardless of how one names the skills associated with the shift, without a doubt the twenty-first-century writing classroom will need to embrace tools, strategies, skills, and dispositions beyond those that crafting only traditional texts requires. This does not mean that teachers must entirely change what they know and do in their classrooms; rather, teachers must explore how their strengths transfer to different tools and emerging genres. Doing so requires that we rethink, oftentimes, the rhetorical situations that we ask students to write within, the audiences we ask them to write for, the products that they produce, and the purposes of their writing.

We understand that this rethinking will not be easy. From contextual factors in the school and community to professional development for teachers, from money to purchase appropriate hardware to the access that students have to that hardware, from the laws that govern child protection to ethical uses of technology, parents, teachers, administrators, and other stakeholders have specific and complex reasons for questioning and sometimes resisting technology. But if digital writing matters, these challenges will need to be addressed and solved. We hope that the questions we raise (and attempt to answer) in this book, as well as the frameworks for thinking about technology use, provide some guidance for the broad range of stakeholders working to integrate digital writing into our classrooms, schools, and communities.

DIGITAL WRITING AND THE NATIONAL WRITING PROJECT

For more than thirty-five years, the NWP has made improving the quality of writing and learning in our nation's schools its central mission. What began in the summer of 1974 as a professional development institute for twenty-five teachers on the University of California campus in Berkeley has evolved into a network of more than two hundred local Writing Project sites in fifty states, the District of Columbia, Puerto Rico, and the U.S. Virgin Islands. Each of these sites operates as a university-school partnership that builds knowledge through the efforts of exemplary teachers and scholars working together. Over its history, the NWP has involved more than two million teachers at urban, rural, and suburban schools in realizing its core goal of improving writing instruction.

From that collective effort, much has been learned about exemplary teaching practices in writing and their impact on students' learning throughout their academic careers. This knowledge has been broadened by three decades of research in the field of composition pedagogy, leading to new understandings about the role of writing in our classrooms that have critical implications for educational reform efforts. Policymakers and school administrators, no less than teachers and parents, can benefit from understanding current trends and issues in the teaching of writing and the vital role it can play in achieving quality and excellence in our classrooms and across the disciplines.

Because Digital Writing Matters describes the current state of technology and writing practices in the United States, with a special focus on interviews with scholars and teachers who are innovating with best practices in teaching writing with technology. Like the original *Because Writing Matters,* this book was conceived by the National Writing Project as a resource for school administrators, educators, and policymakers—in this case, those who want an introduction to how to address the challenge of integrating digital writing practices to improve student writing at all grade levels. The purpose of *Because Digital Writing Matters* is threefold:

1. To make the case that digital writing is a complex activity; more than just a skill, it is a means of interfacing with ideas and with the world, and a mode of thinking and expressing in all grades and disciplines.

2. To examine current trends, best practices, research, and issues in the teaching of digital writing.

3. To offer practical solutions and models for educators and policymakers involved in planning, implementing, and assessing digital writing initiatives and writing programs, as well as those seeking effective staff development for teaching digital writing.

Much like *Because Writing Matters,* this book takes a pragmatic approach—here, to the possibilities of best integrating digital writing practices into our schools and our curricula. The book addresses these core questions:

• Why does digital writing matter?

• What does research say about the teaching of digital writing?

• What are some features of an effective digital writing classroom?

• How can digital writing be used to develop critical thinking?

• How does digital writing fit into learning across disciplines?

• What kind of professional development prepares teachers to teach, create, and distribute digital writing?

• What does a schoolwide digital writing program look like?

• What are fair ways to assess digital writing?

Through stories, examples, and vignettes, *Because Digital Writing Matters* illustrates how educators have used writing with technology in diverse classroom and school settings to enrich learning and provide meaningful writing experiences for students at all grade levels. Given this background and current context, *Because Digital Writing Matters* draws from more than a decade's worth of technology work through the National Writing Project to examine what teachers, administrators, and parents can do to meet the writing challenge in our nation's schools and to equip students with the technology-related communication skills to thrive in our information-rich, high-speed, high-tech culture. It explores the research-based teaching strategies that can improve writing with technology; presents case studies of how effective, schoolwide digital writing initiatives have been designed and sustained; and includes material from a wide range of interviews conducted with current educators in 2008. In short, this book aims to prove that digital writing does matter and to provide a roadmap for teachers and administrators who are implementing digital writing initiatives in their classrooms, schools, and communities.

Chapter One, The Landscape of Digital Writing, elaborates on many of the points made in this introduction about the changing nature of writing in a digital age, and invites teachers to consider questions about why and how to use digital writing with their students.

Chapter Two, Revising the Writing Process: Learning to Write in a Digital World, examines what it has meant and now means to teach and learn digital writing, focusing in particular on how teachers can employ digital writing tools to support students' literacy development and their understanding of the vast amounts of information available to enhance their work as writers.

Chapter Three, Ecologies for Digital Writing, discusses the ways in which physical space, institutional policies, academic expectations, and technology itself continue to shape school culture as teachers, administrators, and students learn how to create effective environments for digital writing.

Chapter Four, Standards and Assessment for Digital Writing, situates the process of digital writing in the larger conversations occurring in our schools related to designing curriculum and to how technology is changing the way we evaluate students on their understanding of that curriculum.

Chapter Five, Professional Development for Digital Writing, outlines a number of key practices that National Writing Project site directors and teacher-leaders are utilizing to help teachers and, in turn, their students become effective digital writers.

We finish with an Afterword, Some Conclusions, Many Beginnings, where we take a look at our rapidly changing work and point to emerging trends in new media, digital writing, and learning.

In sum, this book extends the conversation begun decades ago in the first National Writing Project Invitational Summer Institute: What does it mean to write? What does it mean to be a teacher of writing?

We have, in adding the word "digital" to describe writing, attempted to continue and contribute to that conversation. What does it mean to write digitally? What does it mean to be a teacher of writing in a digital age?

We simply seek to expand our vision of why writing, especially digital writing, matters.

chapter ONE

The Landscape of Digital Writing

> Teenagers' lives are filled with writing. All teens write for school, and 93% of teens say they write for their own pleasure. Most notably, the vast majority of teens have eagerly embraced written communication with their peers as they share messages on their social network pages, in e-mails and instant messages online, and through fast-paced thumb choreography on their cell phones. Parents believe that their children write more as teens than they did at that age. This raises a major question: What, if anything, connects the formal writing teens do and the informal e-communication they exchange on digital screens?
>
> —Lenhart, Arafeh, Smith, and Macgill, 2008, i

Today, students are doing an immense amount of writing—they're blogging; they're text messaging; they're e-mailing; they're updating their status messages, profile information, and live feeds on social networking and other sites; and others are "tweeting" (using microblog spaces and sites like Twitter). Perhaps most interesting in the midst of all this writing students are doing is that they don't often call it "writing." Writing, students note, is something they do *in school*. What they do with computers outside of school is *something else*. As a recent Pew Internet & American Life report on teens and writing noted,

> At the core, the digital age presents a paradox. Most teenagers spend a considerable amount of their life composing texts, but

they do not think that a lot of the material they create electronically is real writing. The act of exchanging e-mails, instant messages, texts, and social network posts is communication that carries the same weight to teens as phone calls and between-class hallway greetings. At the same time that teens disassociate e-communication with "writing," they also strongly believe that good writing is a critical skill to achieving success—and their parents agree. Moreover, teens are filled with insights and critiques of the current state of writing instruction as well as ideas about how to make in-school writing instruction better and more useful. (Lenhart et al., 2008, 2)

A look at the ways in which students are writing today helps clarify the nature of what has been called the "digital revolution." The digital revolution isn't necessarily that we have computers, or that we have computers in schools, or that Internet access has spread so broadly in the United States. For many years, critics of computers in schools have noted that they sit unused at the back of classrooms or, worse yet, that they merely provide "edutainment" for students who cannot engage with typical forms of instruction. (See, for instance, critiques offered by Cuban, 1986, 2001; and Oppenheimer, 2003.) Yet this has not stopped the digital revolution, because the revolution isn't about the tools, but rather how the tools are used. Many technologies have changed writing and writing processes—from chalk to pencils to the typewriter. The networked computer has *dramatically* changed writing and writing processes, and the ways in which people are using the Internet, as well as the sheer numbers of people writing on and with the Web, are having significant social and cultural impact.

This chapter surveys the new digital landscape for writing and examines why digital writing is complex and challenging, for both teachers and students. It identifies and explores some of the complexity that educators and policymakers should understand if they are to develop and sustain effective digital writing programs or curricula. It addresses as well some of the myths and realities surrounding the teaching and learning of digital writing practices, and begins to suggest ways that teachers and administrators can assess how well digital writing is being taught in their schools.

DIGITAL WRITING = WRITING + READING + LISTENING + COLLABORATING

Because Writing Matters presented a compelling vision of writing, arguing first and foremost that writing is hard work. Writers explore and generate ideas, shape their writing for particular audiences and purposes, and work to craft language to convey meaning. Writing well means taking risks, and allowing time to brainstorm and experiment, and later revising and revising (and revising again). When we write, we must be both writer and reader, stepping in and out of a text as we rework it over time for a particular rhetorical situation. As noted in *Because Writing Matters,* this is the recursive and social nature of writing, as years of research in written composition have chronicled.

As the personal computer made its way into the market, many argued that computers would make work tasks—including writing—easier and faster. Certainly, computers allow writers to engage in the work of writing differently, definitely more easily, and perhaps even better: the ease with which multiple drafts can be saved, material can be copied and pasted, and text can be moved around in a document is facilitated by today's word processing programs. Spell-checkers and editing programs can speed up the labor of proofreading, and document design programs can help even novice designers create attractively formatted final products.

But at the same time, computers also provide a more complex space for writing, offering writers a whole new set of options to consider. Computer composition allows for multimedia components such as voice recording, audio, image, video, and more. Along with these media components, writers have access to an array of tools and spaces in which texts can be composed and shared. Writers can shift easily among several different programs including e-mail clients, RSS-feed readers, wikis, blogs, and a number of other increasingly customizable online tools. These online tools allow for virtually instant sharing of texts throughout the writing process, enabling the composing process to be public and interactive from the earliest stages. So for anyone who imagined that computers would make writing easier, the irony is that by making a host of individual tasks easier, computers have dramatically expanded options for writers and have probably made writing, and learning to write, more complex.

Consider this story of Dànielle DeVoss's experience in working on this chapter:

I sit down in front of my computer, coffee in hand. Once my computer has booted up, I launch my applications in the order I tend to use them: WordPerfect (word processing); Eudora (e-mail); Mozilla Firefox (Web browsing and access to Google Docs); Adobe Photoshop (for image editing); Microsoft Word (word processing . . . yes, I use two because although I learned to write with computers using WordPerfect—version 1.0, with its entirely blue screen, before the computer mouse was created!—most of the people I collaborate with use Microsoft Word); and also AIM and Yahoo! Messenger, both for instant messaging (most of the students I work with use AIM, while most of my friends use Yahoo! Messenger).

My Firefox homepage is a customized Google News page, and it loads first. I spend a few moments scanning headlines, and open up a few new tabs—one to check my current eBay bids, one to access the MSU Library's online journals, and another for my Google Docs menu. A couple of people instant-message me to confirm meetings later in the day or to say hi while I'm waiting for my e-mail to come into my inbox. Once my e-mail comes in, I triage, sorting e-mail by priority. Students with questions or concerns get top priority. Administrators with questions or concerns get second priority. Family and friends I save for later in the day. Facebook requests I ignore.

I toggle into WordPerfect and open the "to do" list I update daily and work by religiously. I prioritize the day's items, then toggle into Word to open the first few documents I need to work on: an advising form for a student I will meet with later in the morning, the draft of this chapter, and the table of contents for another book collection I'm working on.

I head to the middle of this chapter, to return to a spot I digitally marked two days earlier—I marked it to return to when my mind was fresher. I think about how I can edit the section, and know I have a good quote that might spark me, embedded in a slideshow presentation I used in a workshop two weeks prior. I launch Microsoft PowerPoint, find the slideshow I'm thinking of, and there's the quote. I copy and paste it into the Word document.

I receive an e-mail from a graduate student working on a project, and send her the files she needs for the document she's working on. A friend of mine sends me a link via instant message, and I take a moment to watch an ad (that he considers hilarious) from the 1980s, now living on YouTube. I pause in remembrance of a YouTube-free world. While I'm in Firefox, I toggle back to my Google Docs tab to check on another document—a conference presentation proposal—I'm working on with two other colleagues. One of the other authors made changes the night before, and I review them, and add a sentence or two. I then head back to Word and continue working on this chapter.

Although many aspects of this digital multitasking might feel new—or even foreign—to writers who learned to write in different environments, it is clear that the work that scaffolds these tasks is similar to the "hard work" of writing in any environment. Composing still depends on phases of planning, reflecting, drafting, and revising, and writers still produce texts for audiences. Collaboration is still a key part of writing well—bouncing ideas off of others and getting feedback across the writing process. And writers still need to learn to manage time and attention to tasks in the face of competing priorities.

But still, there are important differences. In digital spaces, collaboration might happen via e-mail or instant messaging, or it might happen through a course-management system discussion board or some other space for sharing writing. Writing, at every stage of the process, can now be shared across time and space instantaneously to get a prompt response. Thus, the nature of digital writing is such that it both invites and, in some sense, demands instant feedback. Gone are the days when students turned in stacks of essays to a single teacher and were content to wait a day, a week, or a month for feedback. Now students can participate in—or create their own—communities of writers. They are able to stay in touch with others through the RSS readers, social networks, e-mails, mobile phones, and other Internet-enabled tools, in ways that continue to bring text, image, audio, and video together, to share their personal and academic lives. These examples highlight the ways in which digital writing matters to those who are engaged in it.

Thus, the instant communication and always-on connection that students routinely experience in digital environments may be at the root of why students consistently distinguish between the writing that the Pew report called "e-communication" and the writing they are asked to do in school. New digital tools enable a strongly "participatory culture." According to media scholar Henry Jenkins and his colleagues (2006), a participatory culture is one

- With relatively low barriers to artistic expression and civic engagement
- With strong support for creating and sharing one's creations with others
- With some type of informal mentorship whereby what is known by the most experienced is passed along to novices
- Where members believe that their contributions matter
- Where members feel some degree of social connection with one another (at the least they care what other people think about what they have created)

As more and more young people experience this kind of culture around writing and media outside of school, they are likely to bring these interests with them to school. Fortunately for writing teachers, the elements of participatory culture—defined not by the tools but by the experience—can also characterize an effective writing classroom.

RESITUATING THE "DIGITAL GENERATION"

As computer and Internet usage grew throughout the 1990s, policymakers and educators began to focus on the "digital divide": the division in access to technology that separates our schools and children into "haves" and "have nots." As has been reported for years, poorer districts are at a disadvantage in providing the hardware, software, Internet infrastructure, and professional development required to bring effective uses of technology into classrooms. Consistent attention to the digital divide has motivated efforts to expand access, including the substantial provisions of the Telecommunications Act of 1996, which gave the nation the E-rate program.

The law was designed, in part, to help support libraries and schools with the access costs for Internet connectivity. The E-Rate system was introduced within the Act, which allows eligible libraries and schools to purchase crucial infrastructure components. When he signed the 1996 Telecommunications Act into law, President Bill Clinton noted: "Today, the information revolution is spreading light, the light Jefferson spoke about, all across our land and all across the world. It will allow every American child to bring the ideas stored in this reading room into his or her own living room or school room."

Though continued efforts to address the digital divide are critical, many educators are now discussing a second divide: the "digital disconnect," which refers to the disconnect between the current "digital generation" who have grown up in networked environments and their older parents and teachers who have not. The disconnect is what fourteen-year-old "Arthus" discussed in an *EdTechLIVE* Webcast interview with Steve Hargadon, director of the K–12 Open Technologies Initiative at the Consortium for School Networking (CoSN) and founder of the Classroom 2.0 social network. Arthus offered this advice to English teachers: "Stop being so disconnected from the technology . . . learn that there's new ways of learning. It's not about learning the knowledge, but learning to think. All knowledge is a Google away" (Hargadon, 2007).

But schools may not necessarily realize that students hold these views, or agree with the ways in which technology learning is happening at their schools. As reported in *eSchool News* (Prabhu, 2008), Julie Evans, CEO of Project Tomorrow, the group that produces the annual "Speak Up" survey for students, noted that "two-thirds of principals in a recent survey said they believe their school is preparing students to be competitive in the global workforce. But most tech-savvy students didn't share that view." Students reported using less technology in school even as Web 2.0 applications become more ubiquitous outside of school. This digital disconnect is something different from the classic construction of the digital divide. It is not simply about hardware and software (although those are certainly aspects of the disconnect). Instead, the disconnect is about the ways in which teachers and students perceive the application of technology.

Marc Prensky was one of the first to popularize the notion that today's students are the first to have grown up surrounded by digital tools and toys. In his now-famous description (2001), Prensky argues that current students are "digital natives," whereas those who teach them, who learned digital technologies as adults, are "digital immigrants." Digital immigrants, like all immigrants, retain certain "old world" ways of seeing and interacting with their current reality. According to Prensky: "Our students have changed radically. Today's students are no longer the people our educational system was designed to teach" (1). Our "digital native" students access, synthesize, and reply to information in ways that are fundamentally different from what most adults do. Yet we digital immigrants continue to teach "legacy content," or traditional curricula, rather than teaching "future content" such as "software, hardware, robotics, nanotechnology, genomics, etc." as well as "the ethics, politics, sociology, languages and other things that go with them" (4).

The insights of Prensky and many others are useful in pushing educators to consider how digital tools and technologies can transform education, but the distinction between digital natives and digital immigrants is only part of the story. Popular press articles are quick to characterize young people as a homogenous group and to talk about them with labels like "digital natives" and the "digital generation." However, this blanket labeling obscures the very important and fine-grained details related to writing with computers, and the very diverse backgrounds of different writers. Siva Vaidhyanathan, a media studies scholar, argued that this is a "generational myth." In an article in the *Chronicle of Higher Education* (2008, B7), Vaidhyanathan summarizes the clichéd expressions related to how we talk about the "digital youth," and argues that in his years of teaching and being around young people at both public and private universities, he has witnessed a broad, highly variable degree of "comfort with, understanding of, and dexterity with digital technology." Vaidhyanathan warns us that when we talk of a "digital generation," we're leaving out the many, many people without access to digital tools or to the training and support necessary to use them well. It's important to note that in using such labels we create dichotomies and barriers that do a disservice to both teachers and students and may suggest that our new generations of digital natives need only be left alone to learn on their own. These labels, although convenient, generalize and thus obscure the details related to what both students and teachers actually can do with digital technology.

Recent ethnographic research has begun to paint a finer-grained portrait of the digital generation. In one large-scale study led by researcher Mizuko Ito (Ito et al., 2008), a team of ethnographers interviewed over eight hundred youth and young adults and conducted over five thousand hours of online observations as part of a three-year study of youth media use in the United States. Their findings confirm that the digital generation does, in fact, spend tremendous amounts of time using social networking and video-sharing sites, playing online games, and using mobile technologies such as iPods and mobile phones. Yet they also found many differences among young people in their interests, experiences, skills, and knowledge. Rather than suggesting that adults leave the digital generation to themselves to grow and develop in a digital world all their own, these researchers argue for the importance of adult models, mentors, and teachers to help young people learn to navigate the broader digital and social landscape.

> Youths' participation in this networked world suggests new ways of thinking about the role of education. What would it mean to really exploit the potential of the learning opportunities available through online resources and networks? Rather than assuming that education is primarily about preparing for jobs and careers, what would it mean to think of it as a process guiding youths' participation in public life more generally? Finally, what would it mean to enlist help in this endeavor from engaged and diverse publics that are broader than what we traditionally think of as educational and civic institutions?" (Ito et al., 2008, 3)

The twenty-first-century literacy standards documents we are referring to here and, with more detail, in Chapter Four include the following:

Center for Media Literacy, "Literacy for the 21st Century: An Overview & Orientation Guide to Media Literacy Education"
Center for Social Media, "Code of Best Practices in Fair Use for Media Literacy Education"
International Society for Technology in Education, "National Educational Technology Standards (NETS) for Students 2007"
National Council of Teachers of English, "NCTE Framework for 21st Century Curriculum and Assessment"
Partnership for 21st Century Skills, "21st Century Skills Map"

TEACHING WITH AND FOR THE DIGITAL GENERATION

The significant differences in access—access to tools and infrastructure, access to training and support, and access to reflective, educative environments with real mentors—constitute one important reason for schools to take up a conscious focus on digital writing as a mode of learning. For all the ways in which students are situated as the "Net generation" and the "digital generation" and "digital natives," simple access to technology tools will not ensure that students learn to be effective, thoughtful, and ethical digital writers. Teachers are still well positioned to take what Prensky calls the "legacy content" of our curricula and help students move into synthesizing information and creating the "future content." If the proliferation of twenty-first-century literacy standards has shown us anything, it is that educators are concerned about making this happen.

In addition to standards for the "what" of teaching, educators are also rethinking the "how" of teaching with technology so that meaningful learning results. Scholars Punya Mishra and Matthew Koehler (2006) refer to the complex knowledge required for effective teaching with technology as "technological pedagogical content knowledge," or TPACK. Mishra and Koehler argue that teachers have to take a variety of contextual factors into account when choosing how, when, and why to implement a particular technology in their teaching in relation to educational ends. As summarized on the TPACK wiki, these authors state,

> A teacher capable of negotiating these relationships represents a form of expertise different from, and greater than, the knowledge of a disciplinary expert (say a mathematician or a historian), a technology expert (a computer scientist) and a pedagogical

expert (an experienced educator). Effective technology integration for pedagogy around specific subject matter requires developing sensitivity to the dynamic, [transactional] relationship between all three components. (Mishra and Koehler, n.d.)

In short, teachers need to bring a particular expertise that can help them guide their students to become effective digital writers and able learners irrespective of the opportunities they may have outside of school. For teachers, it is not simply a matter of "integrating technology" into the school day, but rather a matter of uncovering the most powerful uses of technology to accomplish learning goals for specific students. To do this, they can create digital environments and experiences to extend their most effective practices into even more powerful learning opportunities for students.

For example, Betty Collum—a fifth-grade teacher at Eupora Elementary School in Eupora, Missouri, and the technology liaison for the University of Mississippi Writing Project—found that her students benefited from learning how to collaborate to improve their writing. Although many of her students had access to some technology tools, such as newer cell phones, they had little experience using networked computers in writing. With a focus on the affordances of collaboration in digital environments, Collum worked with her students to use the online word processing platform Google Docs and to learn about the process of podcasting—creating digital recordings with a simple audio editor, saving it as an MP3 file, and posting it to the class Web site.

For one particular project, she invited her students to create "two-voice tall tales," and they collaborated on everything from their initial drafts through their final podcasts. For Collum, the process required two major steps. First, she began by having students create their tall tale drafts in Google Docs. As she points out, "We are all familiar with word-processing software, as well as with the idea of sending an e-mail attachment to someone for editing and response. Yet Google Docs allows for multiple authors (or 'collaborators') of a document to log in, draft, track the revisions they make, and finally copyedit the work of others." For students, a collaborative tool like this can make the difference between a sequential, text-based, in-class assignment and a lesson in deep revision with an eye toward preparing a text for publication. "It was basically like going through the writing process that my students were already familiar with because we had done it with paper and pencil," states Collum. Students revised their work many times, and Collum believes that the questions they asked each other about the plot and characters in the tall tales contributed to the quality of the drafts they prepared for recording to podcasts.

The second major step was to print the collaboratively authored and edited drafts and to read them aloud. These initial draft podcasts were reviewed by other students before being posted to the Internet: "We got a third-grade teacher to let her kids hear [them], and that was a really major response." Her fifth graders then made final revisions to their scripts and recorded for the final podcasts. Allowing students to use the digital recorders to capture their own voices enhanced revision, as students could move back and forth from their original writing to the recordings throughout the composing process. Once completed, the podcasts were shared on Collum's Web site. She argues for the activity and the publication of the stories by noting that "it is very important for students today to be aware, be familiar with, put their hands on different technology tools that they can use for different reasons." She adds, "Everything that we do, we related to long-term learning."

Although many of her students come to her having never used these digital writing tools, Collum finds that she can expose them to these technologies while also meeting the Mississippi state curriculum standards because she uses them in rich, integrated ways, not as isolated skills. Students in Collum's class learn about more than word processing software and audio-recording tools; they learn how to share their voices through collaboration across the writing process. These tools and experiences do not come from a single packaged program, nor do they happen in a lockstep manner. The tools and processes have been carefully selected by Collum for several reasons:

- They expose students to more generalizable strategies for digital writing that can be used inside and outside of school.
- They cultivate important skills, dispositions, and habits of mind that extend beyond the focused activities themselves.

- They involve students in creating and reflecting on multimodal compositions, helping students learn to manage the intersections of image, voice, and text.
- They involve publishing for real audiences and purposes so that students can experience and learn from the full writing process.

For Collum, it is vital that schools offer opportunities for digital writing as a counter to the digital divide that might otherwise limit students' opportunities and to the digital disconnect that might lead them to disengage with their writing. Her work, though, like the work of writing teachers more generally, addresses a third divide: the divide between consumers of media and creators of media. As computers and Internet access have become more common in our homes, libraries, and neighborhoods, this third digital divide has emerged between those who use computers and Internet access to *consume*—products, information, writing, and more—and those who *produce* such materials. Because digital information is such a large part of our current knowledge economy, the ability to create and to share ideas, arguments, materials, and information across digital spaces will become a more and more crucial skill for individuals, workers, and citizens.

Howard Besser, co-director of the Pacific Bell/UCLA Initiative for 21st Century Literacies, has argued that, while we should still continue to address issues related to access to technology, we should also be paying attention to how we can equip students to be more than passive information consumers.

Besser (2001) argues that as we look at the content available on the Web, we see that there is a *lack of local, contextual, relevant information,* especially for underserved populations; that there are *literacy barriers,* as most online content is written by and for people with strong literacy skills; that there are *language barriers,* in that most Web content is in English; and that there is a *lack of cultural diversity*—that is, it is hard for people to find content produced by other ethnically diverse Americans (a pretty homogenous group produces the majority of Web content). Besser encourages teachers to consider these four factors and to encourage students to be active participants "in the major communication functions of society." He notes that in a digital age, teachers should teach students how to "assemble their writings into forms others will want to read, how to speak publicly . . . [and] how to author and distribute digital works." In the face of the glut of information available through the Internet, there is a real need for young people to learn to thoughtfully create, as well as judiciously consume, Web content.

THE NEW DIGITAL LANDSCAPE: SIMPLER TOOLS FOR A MORE COMPLEX WORLD

Betty Collum's use of Google Docs illustrates significant new options in the digital landscape. Users of this and similar online services, often referred to as "cloud computing," have instant access to the latest versions of the software as well as the opportunity to use the same tools in school and out. Podcasting can be effectively accomplished with simple digital recorders, free or low-cost editing software, and simple distribution Web sites. For schools that previously would have struggled to budget for equipment or puzzled over choices among competing stand-alone word processing programs and platforms, the greater array of Internet-based composing and publishing tools allows for a quicker, more flexible entrée into digital writing.

For many school districts and school boards, these changes can motivate a turnaround in thinking. Originally, computers were slow to enter into classrooms, and when they did, they brought with them significant challenges. Early computer purchases were costly and the machines difficult to use; often, when school districts or individual schools purchased computers, the entire budget went toward the machines themselves, leaving no budget for training and support. In many schools, this resulted in the computers' sitting and gathering dust in the back of the classroom or lab because the teachers had not been provided with the professional development necessary to richly integrate the computer into their practices. In addition, early computers were (comparatively) difficult to use and limited in scope. Amidst the early promotion—some might say hype—of technology in schools, many educators sensed that the machines were not delivering real educational value, and felt that their concerns about the computers' use were not being addressed by policymakers and ed-tech enthusiasts.

In a 2002 article reporting on a technology workshop for teachers of fifth through twelfth grades and their students that enabled them to work together on technology integration and equipped the students to be technology coordinators and helpers in their schools, Dànielle DeVoss and Dickie Selfe (2002) described challenges they observed as teachers worked to integrate computers into their classrooms, lesson plans, and daily work:

- **Inadequate training:** Computers are very complicated tools that in and of themselves don't necessarily make anything easier or faster. For computers to be richly connected to curriculum, a great deal of time and training must be allocated to their integration, and, unfortunately, few schools had (or now have) the means to provide appropriate and adequate training, especially considering how fast technological tools evolve.

- **Shifting notions of texts:** Where does grammar instruction fit, for instance, in slideshow presentations? What happens to the thesis statement in a digital movie? Teachers require new layers of literacies to use and integrate computers in the classroom in ways that do not distract from but instead complement writing practices. And not only do teachers require these literacies, they have to be able to teach and assess them.

- **Shifting notions of literate citizenship:** Students rely on skills that allow them to navigate video games, to search through complex systems, to hack through school- or parent-constructed firewalls, and more. Not surprisingly, teaching new literacies is remarkably difficult in an environment where both technology and digital literacy practices change so rapidly that our schools—including our public schools, and especially our public schools in poor or poorly funded districts—struggle to keep up.

- **An array of student technological skills:** Classrooms are and have always been complicated spaces where a range of abilities are enacted. Technology adds a new layer to these complications, as students bring with them remarkably different technology backgrounds and digital literacy skills.

- **Privacy and personal safety challenges:** The American public has read headlines over and over again in the past fifteen years or so regarding young people "in danger" while participating in online networks. In the classroom, teachers have to negotiate their best practices and the best sites to integrate teaching with the protection of students' identities and privacy in digital spaces.

- **Timing and access:** Teachers who have limited access to computer labs or who have to schedule time in computer labs weeks in advance recognize issues related to timing and access. Just-in-time teaching—having the ability to address student questions, concerns, and writing-related needs as and when needed—is ideal, but when computer lab access is scheduled for the semester or the school year weeks in advance, it's tricky to create a just-in-time environment.

- **Standards and autonomy:** All teachers operate within standards, their implementation, and their assessment. All teachers have to negotiate their classroom and school autonomy within the framework of standards and testing. Because digital writing tools and spaces evolve constantly, no one standard or set of standards will capture entirely or specifically the skills our students need to best equip them in a twenty-first-century world.

- **Public scrutiny:** If teachers have students use authentic, real-world digital tools and spaces in their classrooms, this often means they're having students write to an audience beyond the classroom. In this context, student-produced drafts might be taken out of context, and student work is more visible than it perhaps has been in the past.

New options, such as cloud computing, where composing happens online and is accessed through a simple Web browser, are having an impact on at least some of the challenges noted above. Issues related to particular tools and their uses for digital writing are less often mechanical and more often curricular. As the technologies of digital writing continue to evolve, so too do notions of what is acceptable and ethical in terms of when and how to use technologies. For instance, the notion of copyright has undergone significant consideration in the past decade, as file-sharing sites were started and stopped (and started again). "Fair use" has taken on new meaning in digital writing contexts and an entirely new system of copyright, Creative Commons (creativecommons.org), has emerged to support what scholar Lawrence Lessig (2005, 2008) has called "the remix culture." As a result, the ways in which schools are designing and implementing acceptable use policies (AUPs) continue to push on all these fronts—addressing new hardware and software; uses of the Internet for communicating inside and outside of school; and the ways in which students take information from, repurpose, and post information to the Internet. It used to be that AUPs essentially asked students not to hack the network. Increasingly, they are becoming contracts about how students should act as digital citizens. In short, the landscape of what it means to be a digital writer is increasingly complicated.

But even if the landscape is increasingly complicated, it may also be increasingly fascinating as these are, in fact, the real issues in writing today. The evolution of copyright is not just a school exercise, but is central to how we are coming to understand composition and intellectual property for all writers. Digital citizenship is as relevant outside of school as inside. When Betty Collum's students post podcasts on the Web—and when young people engage in texting, IMing, blogging, and other tasks outlined in the Pew report noted above—they are not merely rehearsing digital writing. They are writing for real audiences and for real purposes.

MEETING THE CHALLENGES OF TEACHING AND LEARNING DIGITAL WRITING

> Writing today is not what it was yesterday. New technologies and new job tasks have changed the meaning of what it means to write and write well. Our educational institutions know they must review what constitutes effective instructional practice to ensure that writing curricula and instructional methods support writing excellence, incorporate technology, and engage and motivate students at all ages.
>
> —Lenhart et al., 2008, 3

So how do we meet the challenge? Colin Lankshear and Michele Knobel (2006) suggest that these types of challenges are less about the technology itself, and more about our mind-set toward its use. They outline two mind-sets toward technology that guide our thinking about effective technology use. In the first mind-set, people assume "that the contemporary world is essentially the way it has been throughout the modern-industrial period, only now it is more technologized, or, alternatively, technologized in a new and very sophisticated way" (33–34). In other words, technology hasn't changed much about the ways in which we perceive our economic, social, and educational systems except that it might allow us to do old things in new ways.

The second mind-set, on the other hand, "assumes that the contemporary world is different in important ways from the world we have known, and that the difference is growing." Enabled by newer literacies and technologies, people are "imagining and exploring how using new technologies can become part of making the world (more) different from how it presently is" (34). As many of the Web 2.0 examples mentioned in this book—such as blogs, wikis, social networks, and photo-sharing sites—show, people are creating, distributing, and remixing the "content" of their lives in ways that were either very difficult or completely impossible before the advent of digital media and the Internet.

If it is true that we are "making the world (more) different from how it presently is," teachers will need the opportunity to learn about and explore this change from inside of it. If digital writing is not, in fact, a "legacy content," then we cannot expect teachers to "inherit it and transmit it"; instead, we continue to learn as we go. As we consider the ways in which digital writing improves student writing overall, we need to consider both the ways in which teachers of writing are introduced to technologies and how teachers of writing address the academic and affective needs of their students, as in the process of creating digital stories.

CREATING DIGITAL STORIES

For Bonnie Kaplan and Clifford Lee, the process of learning how to create digital stories transformed their understanding of what it means to be a teacher of writing as well as of how to engage their students as writers.

Digital storytelling has its roots in the oral tradition of storytelling, and fails to fit into a single definition. In *DigiTales: The Art of Telling Digital*

Stories, Bernajean Porter describes it as engaging with a "palette of technical tools to weave personal tales using images, graphics, music, and sound mixed together with the author's own story voice" (2005, 1). The Center for Digital Storytelling suggests that digital storytelling is a process of "using the tools of digital media to craft, record, share, and value the stories of individuals and communities, in ways that improve all our lives" (n.d.). No matter what the definition, digital storytelling requires teachers and students to shift their thinking about what it means to be a writer, how composing happens, and to whom writing is ultimately addressed.

For Bonnie Kaplan, adjunct faculty member at SUNY–New Paltz and co-director and technology liaison for the Hudson Valley Writing Project, digital storytelling allows teachers the opportunity to talk about a previously nebulous aspect of writing: cultivating voice. Despite the numerous books, articles, and conference presentations about how to help students create a writerly voice, the actual development of such has eluded writing teachers for years. Kaplan suggests that digital storytelling allows writers to express voice in a variety of ways and, in turn, improves their understanding of what it means to be a writer.

Because of the multimedia nature of digital stories, students are able to combine images; video; music; and, quite literally, their own voices into compositions that have an effect more powerful than the written word alone. In workshops with teachers in which they compare traditional forms of writing with students' digital stories, Kaplan claims, "the language [teachers] use to describe the power of voice was much more in depth. There was thought behind it. They were making some immediate connections, visualizing their own classes, and thinking about how their own students could develop their literacy, how this would work in a much more specific way in the development of writing."

Kaplan found that as students moved from writing their stories to gathering media to producing and revising their final stories, teachers felt "this would be such a great hook for them to get kids actually to write." The writing process itself moves from being a fixed set of steps to a more open and recursive journey. "The text can't be fixed," says Kaplan. "If you write a piece by itself, in isolation, you need to be open to its change and transformation."

Similarly, Clifford Lee, formerly a teacher at Life Academy School of Health and Bio Science in Oakland, California, and currently a graduate student in urban education at UCLA, reports that his students became more engaged as writers through the process of digital storytelling. Lee and his colleague Yumi Matsui from the Bay Area Writing Project facilitated a digital storytelling project where students interviewed family and community members to better understand the immigrant experience in America. And this process helped students develop new voices as writers.

One benefit, says Lee, was that "students did multiple revisions on their writing." This occurred for a variety of reasons, some pedagogical and some related to the purposes of and final audiences for the project. For instance, one process Lee asked his students to engage in after getting a rough draft of their story outlined and then timelined was to focus on their spoken narration. He asked them to listen only to their own spoken voices, "just so that students could really focus on how their voice-over narrative drove the story, and [could make sure that] the images and music were complementary to their story." Through this process his students realized that they didn't need to rely on the old writing adage "show don't tell" in every aspect of their story, because their images could speak, too: "Sometimes they started thinking that 'less is more' in their writing, and that the images could drive the story."

Also, Lee noticed that "students went out of their way, on their own, to revise." He continues, "We often force students to make several revisions and have peer edits, but this time we noticed that students were eager to revise it and get feedback from others because they knew that the final project would be shown to an audience that included the person that they interviewed, family members, and community members." This sense of audience and purpose guided students throughout the composing process, and typically paid off in more than a few tears during the exhibition night performances at the school.

For both Kaplan and Lee, their work to create digital stories with students stemmed directly from experiences that each had had in effective professional development. Kaplan suggests that "if you are going to do a workshop, teachers need to have a hands-on experience and leave with something more than, 'Wow, isn't this exciting?'" By focusing on one digital writing process, such as digital storytelling, over a sustained series of professional development sessions, teachers are able to engage in the process and think about how to incorporate this type of writing into their classrooms. Lee credits his willingness to move beyond "typical" uses of technology in his classroom to a weeklong workshop that he attended sponsored by the Bay Area Writing Project and Pearson Education Foundation. For both teachers, lots of time for them to play and develop their own stories led to an understanding of how to use digital storytelling to improve student writing.

SHIFTING RHETORICAL TERRAIN

As noted in the introduction, the WIDE Research Collective (2005) argued that writing instruction must equip students with the tools, skills, and strategies not just to produce traditional texts using computer technology but also to produce documents appropriate to the global and dispersed reach of the Web. This change requires a large-scale shift in the rhetorical situations students are asked to write within, the audiences they write for, the products they produce, and the purposes of their writing. They proposed a set of pedagogical requirements for doing so:

- **Rich contexts for writing**. By this, they mean both spaces that allow students to write with computers and share that writing, and assignments and approaches that encourage students to do so in appropriate ways.

- **A rhetoric that is technological, social, and cultural**. The WIDE Research Collective argued that traditional approaches to audience, context, and purpose certainly carry over into digital realms, but that we must also attend in different and perhaps new ways to the social and cultural contexts of digital writing.

- **An analytical, thoughtful, critical consciousness of technology**. When students live technology-rich lives, and when many technologies become ubiquitous, we must work to remind learners to question technology, to analyze tools, and to carefully select the best tool available for a particular meaning-making task.

- **A "learning how to learn" approach**. Because technologies change and evolve so quickly, it is in our and our students' best interests to teach approaches that transcend specific technologies and can be brought to bear in different contexts and with different tools. In this way, students can change and evolve with technology rather than remain rooted to skills anchored to one particular tool or technology.

- **A recognition of multimodal approaches to writing**. Approaches include writing as text, with images, with audio, with hyperlinks, and much more. Students need to understand how these media work for different audiences and in various contexts and how to layer and juxtapose media to create sophisticated messages.

This is the new "content" that teachers of digital writing must explore with their students, and the first step toward exploring that content for teachers is often the opportunity to work as digital writers themselves and then to receive the support necessary to work and publish in digital environments with their students.

Teachers can't do it alone, of course. Improving digital writing requires a sustained schoolwide effort. Public opinion surveys, interviews with students, and conversations with educators point toward the importance of critically and carefully navigating and putting to use twenty-first-century tools for writing, yet the Internet, the Web, and computer access are still relatively new in our classrooms. For Collum, Kaplan, and Lee, their roles as teachers have changed vis-à-vis the use of digital writing tools; that shift can be incredibly complicated, yet also incredibly rewarding. Thus, in the next chapter, we discuss the ways in which teachers have navigated changes to their roles, and adaptations in their stances toward teaching in tandem with emergent digital technologies.

Revising the Writing Process

LEARNING TO WRITE IN
A DIGITAL WORLD

USING DIGITAL TOOLS TO SUPPORT PROVEN
PRACTICES IN TEACHING WRITING

Over the last fifty years, educators in the field of composition have developed a significant body of knowledge and associated practices that inform the teaching of writing. These practices were outlined in *Because Writing Matters,* and they continue to find support in research (Graham and Perin, 2007; Graham, MacArthur, and Fitzgerald, 2007). Important practices that support writers' growth and development over time fall into three strands of work in the writing classroom:

- Supporting students in the process of writing, including teaching them strategies for planning, revising, and editing their writing as well as processes for working in a community of writers to explore content; to give, receive, and use feedback; and to reflect on their growth over time

- Studying the craft of writing, including analyzing how texts in different media are designed and how they function across genres, purposes, and discourse communities

- Helping students analyze and understand the rhetorical situation for their writing, including how to think about audience, clarify purpose, and work with form and stance in order to cultivate in students the flexibility and strategic thinking that help them address new occasions for writing

Taken together, these strands braid into the diverse approaches teachers use to help students learn to write well. In *Because Writing Matters,* we argued that these approaches make for a strong curriculum in composition when they are paired with attention to helping students *write to learn*—developing the capacity to use writing as a tool for documentation, inquiry, reflection, and analysis of rich content—and when extended and purposeful writing is given plenty of time and attention in an often crowded curriculum.

In Chapter One, we pointed to a range of new digital tools and environments, as well as emerging mind-sets that have affected writing, and we suggested that these are revising our conception of the "writing process." Although this is true, it does not mean that the accumulated body of knowledge and practice about the teaching of writing is now irrelevant. Digital writers at work still move through recursive phases of planning, reflecting, drafting, and revising; they still work hard to develop and edit the content of their writing, to figure out what they think and how they want to communicate. They still produce texts for audiences and make decisions and revisions based on audience reception and the demands of media and form. Perhaps most important, writers still need to learn how best to manage themselves and their writing tasks in the face of competing priorities; but now, competing priorities, such as checking e-mail, sending instant messages, and updating social-network statuses and profiles, are ever-present in the digital environment itself.

It is not surprising that much of what we have known about writing over time also applies to digital writing. Many of the affordances of digital writing environments that we named in Chapter One were developed out of an interest in doing existing composing tasks more efficiently and effectively. Neither collaboration nor joint authorship are new, and so the interest in expanding options for collaboration is a key driver in many groupware environments. It is also not new for writers to take account of the demands of the contexts in which their texts will circulate, whatever they may be, and many new digital tools have grown from the interests writers have in controlling more of the aspects of publication, be it design or circulation or editorial management. And writers have always worked to do research and manage content development for their writing. Digital environments have dramatically expanded writers' ready access to content, even if they have also magnified the challenge of assessing that content.

Supporting students in the process of writing, studying the craft of writing, and helping students analyze and understand the rhetorical situation for their writing thus remain hallmarks of an effective writing curriculum that aims to create reflective, flexible, self-aware writers. In fact, digital tools and environments can help us teach writing more effectively. As Troy Hicks suggests in *The Digital Writing Workshop* (2009), students need to not only "understand the technical aspects of creating hyperlinks, posting to a blog, or collaborating with a wiki, but they need to have the intentional focus as a writer to understand the audience and purpose for which they are writing" (127). Knowing *how* to create a digital text is not the same as knowing *why*, and it is this intentional focus that a good writer must have in order to create engaging texts in *any* environment.

In this chapter we take a look at what happens when teachers begin to integrate digital writing into their classrooms, and we profile teachers who have come to believe that the affordances of new media and new tools have expanded the reach and potential of their writing classrooms. Most of these teachers started small, finding openings that were right for them and their students, and built new practices over time. Eventually, they came to see that digital tools and media had reshaped their teaching in ways they could not have predicted at the onset. Guided by a strong vision of a writing classroom at work, they were able to make the transition into digital environments that benefitted their students. These are the transitions we must pay attention to as we help students learn to write in a digital world.

A Changed Context for Writing: Creating a Wiki with Middle School Students

Anne Moege, an English language arts teacher at Mitchell Middle School in South Dakota and a teacher-consultant with the Dakota Writing Project, saw a way to introduce wikis into a recurring class project. Wikis, which can be used to create collaboratively authored Web sites, struck her as a useful tool for extending the writing that her students did in connection with literature circles. In Moege's approach to literature circles, students read a novel and individually wrote chapter summaries in preparation for discussion. This writing task helped them think through their reading of the novel and participate in discussions, and it helped them improve their skills in writing effective summaries, an important writing task that turned up on assessments and projects throughout the middle school curriculum. By linking summary writing to the real task of preparing for the literature circles, Moege contextualized her teaching about summaries in a real situation with a clear audience and purpose.

As her students began to transfer this classroom routine to a wiki, Moege noticed that students were able to write better summaries when working collaboratively. This raised questions about individual and group capacities. "I had to get rid of the mind frame that if they are not doing it on their own, they're not learning," she states. "'Each kid has to write his or her own summary' might have been my mind frame a while ago. Now, it's 'They can learn a little bit more from each other. They can all offer insight to a chapter. They can collaborate, and they are still learning the same skills.'" Seeing her students work as writers in a digital space shifted Moege's beliefs about what it means to be a writer, and that shift was key to her development as a teacher of digital writing.

What first got Moege's attention was that the collaboratively written summaries were, in fact, better. Because she had carefully situated her teaching of summaries in a purposeful context, the fact that the summaries produced on the wiki were more effective *as summaries* was significant and pointed to the importance of the wiki as a tool for teaching writing. However, improving students' writing on the class wiki was not automatic or instant. Although students were excited about using the wiki, they sometimes had trouble managing their collaborations across locations and time. For other students, writing in a wiki where another student could actually change their words was a new experience and required different ways of working.

Thus a whole host of new skills and dispositions were required to make effective use of the wiki; indeed, this is often the case when we approach any new writing task or tool. Not all students came into Moege's classroom with ready digital skills, or with easy or equal access to technology outside her classroom. As Moege reflected, "The challenge is that some kids were willing to get online at home and do it, and others couldn't. Not all of my kids have access, or they didn't understand all the directions about how to use the wiki." And, of course, there was still the issue of helping middle school students understand what makes a summary effective for particular clusters of audience and purpose.

In short, using a wiki did not eliminate the need for Moege to teach writing, but it did reframe how she taught it. Developing the teaching practices, curriculum, and solutions to the still-relevant issues of access required time and attention, but such development would not have happened if she hadn't been willing to take the first steps with her students. Her assessment? "There is something you can do with technology with your students, even if it seems like a daunting task," she suggests. "Trust them. Even if you are not entirely comfortable with the technology, allow your students to teach you throughout the process."

Moege's experience with introducing summary writing on a wiki involved all the strands of effective practice in the writing classroom. Students still needed to be supported through the writing process, and they needed to learn new skills for productive collaboration in the wiki environment. Students still needed to learn what makes for an effective summary and how to write one. And they still needed to understand and make decisions as writers based on how their summaries would function in the context and with the audience of the classroom literature circles.

THE WRITING CLASSROOM IN TRANSITION

Anne Moege's classroom—and the ways in which she migrated summary writing from the format of the traditional paper written by a single student to that of a collaboratively authored wiki document—is an example of a classroom in transition. Always committed to purposeful, audience-oriented writing, Moege found that digital tools allowed such writing to happen more efficiently and more powerfully than ever before and in a variety of new media. As the authors of *Teaching Writing Using Blogs, Wikis, and Other Digital Tools* (Beach, Anson, Breuch, and Swiss, 2008) explain, digital writing tools can allow us to "deepen our connections and make our learning networks more powerful and real" (ix). This isn't a change that happens overnight, nor does it happen automatically when a writing technology enters the classroom. In fact, technology isn't at the heart of most digital writing practices—the writing itself is, as are the ways in which teachers integrate use of the technology. This is a transition that happens most gracefully when teachers take their best practices in teaching writing, as Moege did, and migrate them to new spaces or tools in ways attentive to how those new spaces or tools might change the writing itself and the processes of writing.

Teaching the Writing Process as Enhanced by Digital Writing Tools

When computers were first introduced into the writing classroom, the machines were often used for grammar drills and spelling quizzes. Mike Palmquist, a professor of English and University Distinguished Teaching Scholar at Colorado State University who codirects the Center for Research on Writing and Communication Technologies, described early applications and their focus on spelling, grammar, and mechanics (2003). He pointed out an important shift that occurred in the mid-1980s, when programs started to emerge that provided prompts for writers to consider audience, or suggestions for brainstorming and drafting. Palmquist characterized this shift as a change from focus-on-tool to focus-on-learner and focus-on-writing. Nonetheless, despite this change in focus, most developers saw the computer as augmenting the teacher or writing coach, helping to individualize the instructional advice that the teacher might give to a writer while still working to scaffold students through a set writing task.

During this time another shift began to occur. As Anne Herrington, Kevin Hodgson, and Charlie Moran report in *Teaching the New Writing: Technology, Change, and Assessment in the 21st-Century Classroom* (2009), early word processing software such as Bank Street Writer, Applewriter, and Writer's Helper situated writers to approach their texts as open to ongoing and easy revision. At the time, this represented a significant affordance. Those who wrote with typewriters were well aware of what was at stake when revising or editing typed copies. Errors in or across pages could destroy a document, and revision typically meant retyping an entire document, not just the section being revised. With word processing software, however, revision was easy. Words, sentences, and chunks could easily be moved around, reorganized, rearranged, and reintegrated, and the whole text would flow forward as a result.

This change in the mechanics of writing fit well with emerging theories of writing instruction that emphasized ongoing revision, peer response, and publishing. Indeed, the ease with which early word processing programs allowed students of all ages to routinely and inexpensively design and print attractive copies of their writing expanded opportunities to have students write for real audiences and purposes. In this way, even prior to the widespread availability of networked computers, the introduction of word processors and desktop publishing can be seen as already having had a significant impact on practice by supporting the growing attention to revision and publication in writing process pedagogies.

Joe Bellino, a teacher of English to speakers of other languages (ESOL) at Montgomery County Public Schools and teacher-consultant with the Maryland Writing Project, developed an early interest in computers and writing because of these early word processing programs. Bellino, who developed a student newspaper for ESOL students called *Silver International* in 1986, found that the editing and publishing capabilities of word processing programs were a tremendous benefit to his language learners. As these software programs developed, they began to include more sophisticated editing, translation, and dictionary tools that created ever more welcoming environments for multilingual student writers. Bellino explains that anything "that allows our learners to get more engaged in a topic can really help a teacher be more effective and get the kids thinking a lot more about what they are doing." Word processing helped students get over some of their language hurdles and focus more on the content of their work. In addition, word processing software helped with legibility and allowed students to self-correct many of their language errors. This was very beneficial in supporting students to begin to work together in peer response groups. With cleaner copies, he found that students could begin focusing on effective peer response, and not just worry about editing.

For Bellino, his inquiry into effective peer response among his students continued as he experimented with different classroom designs, tools, and teaching strategies. In 2006, Writely, an online collaborative word processor that eventually was acquired by Google and became a part of Google Docs, came to his attention. This allowed Bellino to offer his students the writing and editing routines of word processing while adding the benefits of a networked environment. It also allowed students to actually enter into each other's texts and make comments and suggestions, even corrections, in these texts. Students could also review previous drafts to see the impact of their peers' suggestions, and then accept or reject them. With this networked writing space where students could encourage each other to write—through collaboration and real-time response—Bellino found that his students began to revise even more effectively.

The transition to more collaborative writing happened in a few ways. First, students were able to learn different approaches to writing from others. Certain students became "little teachers," Bellino reports, and they reminded others about instructions he had given the class during minilessons, such as to have a topic sentence or to use details. Second, the sense of audience moved beyond the teacher, as students were sharing with their peers and could easily publish to the wider Internet. Peer response became even more critical to students' writing process because students wanted to get their thoughts and words just right. Summarizing his beliefs about how Google Docs enhanced his class, Bellino shares the expectations that he had for his students: "I expected them to have an immediate audience, to get that encouragement, and to do their best to learn from each other."

Although improvements in students' work were not immediate, with time and practice they did come. He and his coteacher Ailish Zompa worked together on a teacher research project and concluded that "it wasn't in the individual draft where you would see as much change as you would over multiple drafts and different assignments. You could compare the first assignment to the last assignment and see dramatic improvement in terms of length, in terms of ideas, where the students would really try to be thoughtful in their writing in terms of organization." By looking at revisions across the year and over multiple assignments, students were also able to recognize their growth as writers. And with all of their work easily accessible online, they had an ongoing archive for examination and reflection.

Digital Tools to Support Listening and Speaking Skills

Just as the process of writing and revising has cumulative effects over time, listening and speaking are also important, particularly for English language learners. Digital tools can play a role with these language processes too. For Robert Rivera-Amezola, fourth-grade teacher at Francis E. Willard Elementary School in Philadelphia, and a teacher-consultant with the Philadelphia Writing Project, inviting his English language learners to literally share their voices through digital audio recording made a difference in their perceptions of themselves as readers and writers, listeners and speakers.

"Kids who are at an emergent level of language acquisition may be challenged to write in English, and can barely pronounce sounds, but practicing some of the sounds with digital recording is useful," says Rivera-Amezola. Moreover, it helps him assess comprehension when students record their responses to reading as a podcast: "It is a great way to assess how much kids understand what they are reading, based upon the sound effects they put into their podcasts." In making choices about sound effects, "they may not be able to verbally communicate everything that they understand, but the way they produce their recording tells you a lot about where they are coming from and how much they have acquired."

For another assignment, students create slideshow presentations, and Rivera-Amezola then has them narrate their slideshows using Apple's GarageBand software. Students write across different modalities, and Rivera-Amezola has them participate in the writing process of brainstorming, drafting, revising, and editing. The process appeals to all of his students because of the variety of composing tasks. "What I want to bridge is what is happening in the world today in terms of communication and what we believe should happen in the classroom," he declares. "I would suspect that a lot of these kids will grow up not really writing [in a traditional sense], but having to learn to communicate in modalities that weren't available to us when we were kids." And, he believes, all this composing helps them learn English.

Taking these principles and putting them into action is an important part of Rivera-Amezola's digital writing pedagogy. He works with students and community partners in local neighborhoods to create "Need and Deed" projects, in which students participate in service learning and then document their work using digital writing tools such as digital voice recorders and cameras. He feels that he is helping students prepare for jobs that are yet to be invented, teaching them how to collaborate, and, as important, supporting them in communicating beyond the classroom through technology. Digital writing helps students learn about diversity and learn how to problem solve: "It's about communicating with all kinds of different people who may be dissimilar to you but are working on a similar goal."

Similarly, for Bellino, the reasons to use technology are clear: "From my perspective, it's not just something that helps kids improve their writing; it's something that helps the teachers be more effective teachers. And that has to have a payback to the kids."

Writing Process Strategies as Enhanced by Digital Writing Tools

The benefits Bellino and Rivera-Amezola have witnessed for their English language learners are, of course, not limited to this population of students. What these examples illustrate is not only that our best practices in teaching writing transcend specific technologies but also that technologies can enhance our practices. Following the examples of Moege, Bellino, and Rivera-Amezola, who sought to extend their most effective practices in the teaching of writing by incorporating new digital tools, we can find a wide range of uses for digital tools in the writing classroom.

A Sampler of Writing Process Strategies as Enhanced by Digital Tools

Audience and identity: Writers present an identity and address audiences, both real and imaginary, in their work. Audiences may include the writer him- or herself, the teacher, peers, friends, the school, the community, or the public at large. With digital writing, audiences are potentially much broader and can be contributors to the writing, especially when teachers provide students with opportunities to engage in online communities that encourage posting and response to writing. Communities such as Youth Voices, discussed in Chapter Three; blogging networks; or social networking sites help writers meet and interact with audiences. In relation to those audiences, students begin to see how writers craft and present multiple identities in their writing and link that to the management of identities through profiles, links, and design.

Writing processes: Writers go through cycles of activity when they compose. These are sometimes described as cycles of planning and revising (generating ideas, setting goals, and organizing), or they can be categorized as activities, such as prewriting, drafting, revising, and editing. Digital writing spaces, like word processing software, facilitate the methods by which writers can easily revise and edit by allowing multiple drafts to be saved and by providing commenting features. Moreover, as digital writing tools become more ubiquitous—through applications such as Google Docs that are accessible on Internet ready cell phones—a writer's process can move from idea to idea, machine to machine, space to space, and time to time in ways that allow writing to happen almost everywhere.

Prewriting and researching: Prewriting includes any planning activity that helps writers invent content and generate ideas. For instance, some computer programs and Web sites facilitate planning by providing mapping and outlining tools. Additionally, digital writers may capture ideas through digital voice recorders or by sending themselves e-mails or text messages when an idea strikes. While mapping and outlining are popular means of prewriting, visualization tools such as Inspiration, Bubbl.us, Wordle.net, or Magnetic Poetry allow writers to play with words in creative ways, thus inspiring ideas for further writing. Writers may also gather collections of links by subscribing to relevant RSS feeds and by using social bookmarking tools such as Del.icio.us or Diigo to gather URLs of Web sites they would like to access later or share with others.

Freewriting and collecting: Peter Elbow (1998a; 1998b) has defined *freewriting* as private, nonstop writing—putting words on the screen without worrying about the constraints of grammar or staying on topic. The goals are to build fluency and generate material that can be used later for more formal writing occasions. One tried-and-true freewriting technique writers use to alleviate "blank screen anxiety" or writer's block is to turn off the computer monitor and just begin typing. Freewriting generates a wealth of material and starter texts that can be collected into a journal and later mined for projects. In digital writing, writers may maintain private blogs or Twitter accounts to serve as personal writing notebooks in which they record ideas that they can access later. In addition, many blogging environments allow writers to control their posts, to make some public and others private, much like a personal journal.

Drafting: Drafting is the stage when the writer begins to develop content through sustained production of prose. Although the formal aspects of the finished piece may not yet be of key concern, the writing begins to take shape at this stage, and

(continued)

structure, flow, and organization start to emerge. Word processing software has always allowed writers to save multiple versions of their drafts as they move from prewriting to freewriting and into drafting. Newer digital writing tools, such as on-line word processing programs and wikis, automatically track changes as new versions are saved and allow comparisons among drafts. Also, by its very nature, word processing software allows writers to manipulate and remove text to easily see how changes affect the overall flow of the piece.

Revising: When revising, writers approach a rough draft with an editorial eye, deleting extraneous content, focusing the material, determining where to add more detail, and so forth. Although usually performed by the writer, revision is often supported by review, comments, and feedback from others. Digital spaces for sharing allow writers to post drafts and to solicit feedback and suggestions for revision. In all these steps of the revision process, tools such as highlighting and commenting allow users to indicate specific sections of the text that they are seeking response to or offering comments upon, thus making the entire process more efficient for writers and responders. Some environments allow commenting to be multimodal. VoiceThread, for example, allows for voice comments as well as offering drawing and annotation tools. Voice conference services like chat rooms or YackPack also allow for synchronous and asynchronous conferencing.

Editing: Some writers edit while they revise, and other writers edit when they have almost-done drafts that they want to polish and finalize. Editing usually involves line edits and proofreading, focusing on mechanics, spelling, punctuation, and other writing conventions. Word processing applications, among other digital tools, can help during this stage of writing, as most have built-in grammar- and spell-checkers. In addition, wikis, Google Docs, and word processing programs allow writers to track editing changes for later study and reflection.

Publishing: Writing teachers have worked in different ways to support student publication, seeing that it can have an impact on student engagement and create real contexts for writing. Digital tools and environments dramatically expand publication opportunities for students by allowing texts of all sorts to be distributed on the Internet easily and at minimal cost. Blogs, Web sites, wikis, and profile pages are all ways to publish. Podcasts and digital stories are products that engage students as creators and can be easily made public on the Web. Publication can also help students see and create emergent forms by looking at texts from a perspective of publication—for example, considering how a personal bookmark collection can become an annotated bibliography or a series of trip photos can be made into a travel essay.

Multigenre and multimodal writing: In order to encourage flexibility and to build awareness of the demands of differing genres and situations, writing teachers often design assignments that require students to create multigenre projects, an approach in which writers create multiple texts related to a similar topic, choosing different audiences, purposes, and genres in which to represent their work. For instance, a multigenre project on a historical figure may be written in the form of an autobiographical sketch, a newspaper article about the figure, a letter from that figure to a significant other, and a one-act play highlighting an event in that figure's life. Multimedia writing tools such as slideshow software, Web site creation programs, and digital movie or audio editing applications help expand the options for such assignments and introduce opportunities to reflect on what happens when content is expressed in different modes.

Electronic portfolio: As a compilation of a writer's work, displayed in the form of a Web site, slideshow, or other form of multimedia, electronic portfolios allow writers to present not only textual documents but also audio work, video work, and multimedia compositions. Electronic portfolios also allow writers to edit, add to, or otherwise change their materials as they see fit—a staple of using portfolios in a process writing pedagogy—allowing writers to maintain a sense of ownership over the work they are presenting for assessment. This ability to revise is also a staple of writing pedagogy that encourages writing as craft and as process, and that encourages writers to revise and edit pieces as "living documents," a process made even easier through the use of collaborative word processors, wikis, and other digital writing tools.

THE WRITING PROCESS IN THE INFORMATION AGE

In many ways, then, digital tools allow us to improve and extend our writing pedagogy. We turn now to areas where new digital tools are having an even larger impact on writing—and therefore on the teaching of writing. Few elements of writing practice have been affected as deeply by new digital tools as the processes of inquiry, research, and content development. From the abilities of search engines to the numerous collections of digitized archives of print material to the massive and collaboratively produced Wikipedia, the availability, management, distribution, and redistribution of information around the world has been radically transformed by the Internet and networked computers. Writing classrooms are an important location to explore the idea of "information literacy" as well as "media literacy" and to support students in discovering strategies they can use to analyze resources related to the topics on which they are writing. Some of these are tasks we've always engaged in, although our tools used to be highlighters, reference cards, index cards, and lessons in attribution. But some of our tasks are also dauntingly new, such as thinking about the use and reuse of images, text, music, and sound when so much is now available to combine across media, and redistributable at the click of a button. Now we have the responsibility to teach students how to swim in the sea of information and media that is the Internet.

Writing teachers are not alone in this responsibility, of course. In his essay "The Next Digital Divides," Howard Besser (2001) calls attention to librarians as leaders in information literacy, and Joyce Valenza, Library Information Specialist for Springfield Township High School in Erdenheim, Pennsylvania, is one of those leaders. Valenza's teaching and work focus on changes in information literacy and research skills that are intertwined with what it means to be a digital writer. "Writing is the basis of all student communication," she believes. "So, even if we are talking a lot about multimedia tools, it all has to do with writing. The ease with which we can write has been amazingly facilitated [by technology]." As an award-winning blogger, published author, and presenter on topics related to libraries, technology, and education, Valenza practices what she teaches each day. From her NeverEndingSearch blog (see Web Resources) to her personal homepage (Valenza, n.d.) and library wiki site (see Web Resources, Springfield), Valenza shows the changing landscape of how information is produced and distributed, and generously shares her knowledge with students, teachers, and other librarians.

As a specialist in "information," Valenza understands that we now need to teach students dramatically different ways of searching for, managing, and assessing information. For example, she works with students to create "path finders" with wikis (using Wikispaces), build personalized homepages using homepage generators such as Pageflakes, and subscribe to RSS feeds. Her path menu Web page provides an example and gives them a place to start. As teachers and students ask for more and more Web-based sources, she creates new path finders on subjects ranging from typical school topics, such as grammar, colonial America, the planets, social issues, and the natural elements, to topics focused on newer literacies, such as access to copyright-friendly images and sounds and primary sources available in full-text versions online. As students do their research, she invites them to add quality links and to help build resources.

While supporting student researchers throughout their entire school careers, Valenza makes specific note of how she works with teachers and their students during the senior seminar. As in many high schools, seniors are expected to create a culminating research project that synthesizes information gathered from a variety of sources into a final presentation. Digital writing tools permeate the research process, helping students keep their information organized and their writing processes fluid.

The research process begins when students create their personal iGoogle pages, which have their teachers' wikis, RSS feeds from the library, other RSS feeds related to their topics, calendars, and to-do lists. Valenza describes the change in her own thinking about how to have students begin the research process:

> I used to believe, maybe four or five years ago, that everybody should use my homepage as their homepage. And that was really arrogant. If I can own a tiny piece of real estate on their home screen, which is now iGoogle, and I can do that just through a bookmark, that is space enough for me. Really, what it is, and I would never label it that, because it would take all the coolness away, is a "personal information portal." We're teaching kids to push information [by utilizing RSS] rather than pull it [by doing searches].

Once the information starts flowing, students need to keep it organized. Valenza works with teachers to help students create blogs, in which they outline their research process and reflect on what they have found and how they found it. Students' blogging, says Valenza, allows teachers to see students' thinking, and, when necessary, step in: "We would not only interact, but intervene, because the research process and writing are very chaotic. When you add research to the writing process, it gets crazier." In this way, blogs serve much the same purpose as researchers' notebooks or reflective field memos, but their public nature allows for a strong community of practice to emerge.

She mentions a library study that shows how students progress, and regress, in the research process: students move from confidence to frustration, and teachers, librarians, and media specialists can be there to help them while, for instance, monitoring their blogs. "What happens is, if I can get in there, and a student is writing about girls and body image, I can say, 'I love what you are writing about. I think you've got some great ideas. And have you seen *Reviving Ophelia*?'" Then she helps the students identify new resources. She also notes that teachers can go back to the students' posts and use them as models. Showing what one student has done that is working well—a tried-and-true aspect of the writing workshop approach— allows other students to gain insight into the research process. Blogging throughout the research process is a way to keep track of ideas and reflect on what was found, and a student can turn this initial writing into the basis for a draft of the research paper.

Students are invited to use a variety of other free Web-based and open-source tools to manage the research process and create their final products. Some keep virtual "notecards" in Google Notebook. Mind-mapping tools, office suite software, and other productivity tools are outlined on one of Valenza's wiki pages, and students are welcome to use as many, or as few, as are useful to them. Valenza also supports her students with a link to the Web site Copyright-Friendly and *Copyleft* Images and Sound (Mostly!) for Use in Media Projects and Web Pages, Blogs, Wikis, etc. (n.d.) at copyright-friendly.wikispaces.com/. The term *copyleft*, which is a play on *copyright*, refers to a form of licensing that is focused on fair use; makes a resource free; and requires all modified, adapted, and remixed versions to be free as well. To address the complicated set of literacies involved in using copyright and copyleft materials, Valenza's Web site includes a link for students to get more guidance from the *Code of Best Practices in Fair Use for Media Literacy Education*, an excellent guide for both teachers and students in this complicated era of use, reuse, attribution, and distribution.

Valenza wholeheartedly supports the idea of using Web-based bibliographic tools, such as NoodleTools. Her reasoning is straightforward: removing the "icky" part of citation generation allows kids to "really focus on the content. Honestly, finding the best sources is what matters, not worrying about where the colon goes." Thus, she concludes, if you have a tool that will generate citations for you, then you don't have to spend most of your time working on formatting. Instead, you can work on what matters as a writer: communicating with your audience.

EMBRACING THE CHANGES IN A TIME OF TRANSITION

As research institutions, museums, libraries, governments, and publishers move to digitize their holdings and circulate ever more information through the Internet, new processes for information storage, retrieval, and circulation will transform the processes of research and the practices for teaching research. Routines built around index cards and markers will be set aside or, at the very least, disrupted. For classrooms making the transition to digital writing, some emergent practices are likely to disrupt current ideas and practices in teaching the writing process.

For example, it has been conventional to talk in terms of composing and revising multiple drafts in the writing classroom. But in new digital environments, what is a draft, exactly? Is a draft when the computer saves our work automatically? When we choose to share a version with colleagues? Or is a "draft" something else? What is it when we revise a paragraph in an existing blog entry not because we want to "say it better," but because we want to improve the visual design of the piece by including an important graphic that then forces our text to wrap awkwardly? Similarly, how will our understanding of conventional forms such as the essay evolve as qualities such as "unity" give way to forms that emphasize "mash-ups" or what Jason Ohler (2009) has called "media collage"? What is the relationship between how we talk about organization in text and navigation on a Web site or blog?

These sorts of questions will emerge from the experience of writing in digital environments, and that experience will push us, collectively, to build new knowledge that will inform the teaching of writing. It is, perhaps, most important that we continue to write and that we experience many diverse opportunities for digital writing so that we can build digital fluency. Digital fluency, Ohler writes, "is much more of a perspective than a technical skill set. Teachers who are truly digitally fluent will blend creativity and innovation into lesson plans, assignments, and projects and understand the role the digital tools can play in creating academic expectations that are authentically connected, both locally and globally, to their students' lives" (13). Classrooms in transition may emphasize a medley of strategies, such as these:

- Provide writers with a wide range of playful, low-stakes opportunities to brainstorm, freewrite, draft, compose, and edit (with text, graphics, sound, and still and moving images) using computers, digital tools, communication technologies, and network spaces to improve their skill and flexibility as writers. Explore the wide range of mind-mapping, office suite, image-editing, audio-editing, and video-creation tools that can support this work, many of which are available to schools for free.

- Build online searches, critical reading, and information literacy into classroom routines, helping students articulate and apply evaluative criteria to assess the validity and credibility of research findings. Create "portals" for online activities—pages of links for students to focus on— and engage students in performing online research using Web-based search engines and online databases. Pose problems, puzzles, or questions and invite students to think of innovative ways to use technologies to address these queries.

- Create room for students to work both individually and collaboratively with a variety of media to design, develop, publish, and present original ideas to multiple audiences (for example, slideshow presentations, newsletters, Web sites, digital movies). Have students explore different information and communication technologies and choose the best technology to facilitate the task at hand and the situation to which they are responding.

- Invite students to participate in teaching. In technology-rich classrooms, there will always be a range of students with a broad and often diverse set of technology-related skills, and students are often excellent teachers or mentors. Through the process of teaching and learning from each other and sharing experiences as writers, students will learn to make knowledge from their experiences in digital environments and transfer that knowledge to new problems and challenges.

- Help students to understand *both* writing and technology as complex, socially situated, and political tools through which humans act and make meaning. Approach each different technology as a learning experience; prepare students to be good learners and critical thinkers who can take strategies and apply them in different situations with different tools.

Keeping pace with technological change sometimes feels overwhelming. But good teaching practices—as the stories we have included in this chapter demonstrate—are far more important than any changes in technologies. "Digital" is simply the way we write today. As Troy Hicks proposes in *The Digital Writing Workshop* (2009),

> If we engage students in real writing tasks and we use technology in such a way that it complements their innate need to find purposes and audiences for their work, we can have them engaged in a digital writing process that focuses first on the writer, then on the writing, and lastly on the technology. As we shift our attention from the technology back to the writer, we begin to take the stance of not just integrating computers or using a particular program and begin to think about how to structure our digital writing workshop. (8)

While digital writing tools will continue to have an impact on our classrooms and on our understanding of the writing process, by holding tight to core principles that have informed the writing process movement—and, indeed, informed the work of thousands of writing teachers over the past three decades—we can maintain a solid pedagogical base despite rapid changes in technology. With digital writing at the center, we can still work to support students in the process of writing, study the craft of writing, and help students analyze and understand the rhetorical situation for their writing. To do so requires a robust infrastructure for teaching digital writing, so in the next chapter we move into a discussion about how to foster and sustain healthy "technological ecologies" in which these practices can occur and flourish.

chapter THREE

Ecologies for
Digital Writing

In the natural environment, small changes can be powerful. Changes in temperature, the introduction of a new species, or the rerouting of a water source can have long-lasting effects. This is true in the classroom environment as well. Educators are often comfortable thinking about his or her school, classroom, or other setting as an environment: a social environment, an academic environment, a work environment. The word *environment* points to the interrelatedness of the different elements of educational settings. In this chapter, we consider how we might expand that way of thinking to include the environment for digital writing: a concept we call the *digital ecology*. More than ever before, the proliferation of tools, infrastructures, and policies for digital writing demands that writing teachers work to shape a healthy and sustainable ecology for digital writing.

IN ECOLOGY SMALL CHANGES MEAN BIG RESULTS

For Renee Webster, a first-grade teacher in Perry, Michigan, and co-director of the Red Cedar Writing Project at Michigan State University, the introduction of a small set of digital voice recorders into her classroom led to significant new opportunities for her first-grade writers. As novice writers, six-year-olds work hard to master the mechanics of alphabetic literacy. For Webster, it is important to also let students experience the larger purposes of writing. "I want to have them know that part of the writing process is communicating, and we want to share our stories with other people," says Webster. "This is where the digital recorders come in."

Before the end of the first week of school, Webster invites her students to compose personal narratives, then helps them capture these as audio files with a digital voice recorder and, finally, upload them to the class Web site. Each story is then accessible through the Internet, and students are able to share their memoirs with their parents—as well as anyone else with Internet access, such as a relative who lives far away. The effect? Long before students are able to compose these stories independently with pencil and paper, they are able to perceive themselves as composers, as writers. When children use digital voice recorders to "capture stories in their own voice," Webster observes, "the child feels like a writer. They are so excited when they hear themselves reading their piece. It's like, 'Yeah, I wrote that. That's my story. I'm a writer!'"

As a part of inviting students to share their voices online, Webster needed to teach them about how to manage files and organize their digital work. In order to put their work online, Webster worked with her district technology coordinator to revisit the district's Acceptable Use Policy (AUP). Previously, teachers had to get parental permission separately each time they wanted to post students' work online; after some planning with her technology coordinator, Webster was able to create an option for full parental permission at the beginning of the school year. That allowed her to work with families via the Internet all year long without needing to secure consent for every artifact. This change allowed Webster to invite her students to become routine digital ethnographers of classroom practice throughout the year. Finally, she had to rethink how to use the limited time she was given in the computer lab. Instead of simply practicing keyboarding, students began learning early how to share files on the school network and upload files to the class Web site. Webster believes that helping them become independent led to big changes in their thinking. "They feel agency and responsibility, even as six-year-olds—that their job in school is to be thinkers and to have personal intentions for doing and learning," she observes.

In Webster's classroom, digital writing is not a trade-off from more traditional writing practices for emergent writers; indeed, learning to write in conventional ways is still vitally important for Webster's first graders. But the addition of the digital audio work has proved to be a powerful enhancement to her teaching. "I see that they have to have the digital exposure as much as they need the pencil paper work at encoding their text. If I can't engage them, I can't teach them no matter how good the tools and strategies are that I have. Having the option of digital media helps me better engage all of the kids." She is also convinced that they grow as writers: "They learn to try new things as writers, not only from hearing their own story played back, but also from hearing somebody else's story. They learn elements of author's craft, such as how to use dialogue or repetition, by listening to how their peers have employed the strategies introduced in class minilessons."

Many of the benefits Webster has seen stem from having integrated this digital work routinely into her classroom and her curriculum. "By entering the digital world, you are taking down the walls, opening up your classroom, and making almost anything possible," she concludes. "Because if students come to you and want to try something, you can figure out a way to do it. And that's really exciting." The excitement of being able to create new projects, follow student interests, and invite them to dream big is supported by having appropriate digital tools at the ready as part of the classroom environment.

This is the kind of environment that we call a healthy digital ecology for writing.

CRAFTING A HEALTHY DIGITAL ECOLOGY

Crafting a healthy ecology for digital writing is an important part of our teaching practice. The concept of ecology is a rich one for thinking about the larger context in which digital writers compose. Coined by biologists in the late 1800s to refer to the holistic study of the relationship of living organisms to their environments, the term *ecology* has been used by scholars such as Bonnie Nardi and Vicki O'Day to describe the technology environments in which we work. As Nardi and O'Day (1999) explained in *Information Ecologies: Teaching Technology with Heart,* "We see technology as part of an ecology, surrounded by a dense network of relationships in local environments" (27). Nardi and O'Day remind us to take account of not only the human actors involved in technology work but also the "non-human" actors that both invisibly and visibly shape the work that we do and the way we do it.

Some of the more common elements of a digital ecology fall under the heading of technology infrastructures:

- Computers; software; hardware; and peripherals (like digital cameras, scanners, and printers)
- Intranets or local networks, Internet/Web access (and configurations and firewalls that either support or infringe upon network access), and adequate Internet bandwidth for uploading and downloading online content
- Storage spaces, both local (hard drives) and remote (server space)
- The physical layout and arrangement of computer-rich spaces, including the availability of computers for teaching purposes (for example, having computers in a classroom; bringing students to a computer lab)

Other elements of a digital ecology are less visible, but no less significant. These include the ethical, legal, and policy environments that surround student participation in the Internet and the design of online spaces. These elements of a technology infrastructure would be matters of common concern for any of the technology specialists who support schools and universities, and increasingly for architects and building supervisors. What makes them matters of concern for teachers of digital writing becomes clear when we view these elements as part of the overall learning environment—the ecology. Ecological principles tell us that organisms adapt to and influence their environments; likewise, writers adapt to and influence their digital environments. Understanding, improving, and shaping a healthy digital ecology is part of teaching digital writing.

This chapter attends to three components crucial for a healthy ecology in which effective digital writing practices can flourish:

- The physical space for digital writing
- The ethical, legal, and policy environments for digital writing
- Online environments for digital writing

We conclude with a look at technology stewardship. Certainly, these are not all the components necessary for robust digital writing work, but they are, we believe, key components that foster effective practices for teaching digital writing.

COMPONENT ONE OF A HEALTHY DIGITAL ECOLOGY: PHYSICAL SPACE FOR DIGITAL WRITING

Most teachers are keenly interested in the physical environments of their classrooms, making a range of decisions about arrangement and design with the goal of fostering interaction and learning. The introduction of technology, however, presents a special problem. Bulky equipment, awkwardly placed electrical outlets, and all that wiring can pose challenges to design. Even teachers who give careful attention to the design of their classrooms back off from making decisions about technology-rich spaces. Given these challenges, it is good to remember how far we have come over the last few decades. Pamela Childers—a former public high school teacher and writing center director who currently serves as the Caldwell Chair of Composition at The McCallie School—described working in 1983 in Red Bank Regional High School in Little Silver, New Jersey, with an Osborne 1 computer. At twenty-five pounds or so, the Osborne was widely hailed as the first "portable" computer. Childers (2004) said,

> Once I mastered the basics . . . and memorized all the mnemonics I could muster to learn the commands to save and print (logical and KS for keep and save; logical and KP for keep and print), I was ready to conquer the world of computers with students in our English classes and in the writing center.

Students loved volunteering to cover the writing center room while I was teaching because they could write on the computer and save their work to the 5-inch floppy disk in Drive B, while the Image disk stayed in Drive A. They didn't seem to mind that the built-in gray monitor was only about six inches in diameter. However, I certainly minded carrying the 27-pound computer down the steep metal stairs each Friday to connect to the media center printer, print out student files as well as my own files, and then carry the Osborne and the papers back up the steps. I still think my one arm is longer than the other. These now-amusing first experiences allow me to reflect on and realize the constant challenge of balancing the drawbacks and benefits of using technology. (473)

In comparison with scenes like this, a purpose-built computer lab outfitted with desktop machines that did not require heavy lifting would be a dream come true. So it is not surprising that, where possible, available rooms were adapted to create early computer labs. In her essay, Childers describes the writing center's move from what was essentially a closet to a walk-through space on the first floor with two stationary computers and a printer.

Despite the many changes in technology infrastructure since the days of the Osborne, many of our schools' and institutions' computer labs still look much the way they did when they were first built. The computers are often situated in rows—a design that replicates a traditional, lecture-style mode of teaching, where the teacher is the authority in the room and lectures from the front (see Figure 3.1 for a sample floor plan of a typical computer classroom). Students face the teacher as well as the backs of the heads of the students in front of them. Although students come to class in groups, these spaces facilitate individual, isolated learning that is the antithesis of the kind of collaboration and flexibility that networked computers can foster.

There are other elements to this common lab design that are troubling. In the floor plan here, for example, there is only one entrance per row of computers; students at stations 5, 9, 13, 17, 21, 25, and 29 sit next to a wall. The tight allocation of space means that movement is restricted, and it is almost impossible to ask students to work together. Monitors block students

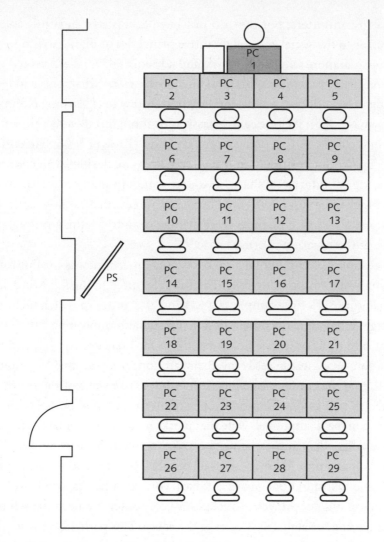

Figure 3.1 Computer Classroom Setup 1

from one another, and a lack of desk space means that they would find it difficult to work with the array of tools writers use—notes, scratch paper, storage devices—around them. These problems are compounded by the physical place being "locked down" in a very real sense: wires, cables, computers, and monitors running the length of these rows are bolted to each other to prevent theft. In computer labs such as these, students may have access to computers, but they do not have access to a healthy ecology conducive to the social and collaborative principles of digital writing.

More and more scholars, teachers, and administrators have accepted that learning spaces should be adapted to how people learn, what tools and technologies are used for teaching and learning, and who is learning (Johnson and Lomas, 2005). Well-designed classrooms thoughtfully integrate online learning, collaboration, and content creation (Brown, 2005; November, 2007). Spaces that foster a healthy digital ecology are flexible, with common technological interfaces; shared resources; and, in many cases, seamless technology integration (Valenti, 2005). Resources such as those collected by Educause (see Web Resources) are helping institutions think through the design of these learning-focused spaces.

In response, computer labs are becoming environments for improved learning—and improved *writing*. The room featured in the following floor plan (Figure 3.2), for example, is a writing classroom in which technical writing, Web design, document design, layout, and publishing courses are taught, and which was specifically created to facilitate group work and collaboration. Students can easily roll chairs around, group around a computer, or gather at the conference table in the center. The walls of the room are painted in rich colors—burgundy, pumpkin orange, and butter yellow— rather than the institutional white that marks most computer labs. The conference table offers buckets of markers, colored pencils, pens, stickers, and other tools and toys. There are several bookshelves in the room, packed with practical and inspirational materials. Each computer has its own hard drive for storing student projects; almost every computer has been named by a student, using the alphabet stickers in the room. This particular campus has a universal network, with shared software, but the instructors argued early on for the rights to install software locally on these machines.

Another flexibly designed computer classroom, shown in Figure 3.3, provides for a student-centered, production-oriented, writing-intensive, and technology-immersive space for individual student work, group work, and small- and large-group discussion. The space also provides for ease of movement and discussion, and offers flexible presentation space for students and instructors. In this room, computers are not provided, as students are expected to bring their own laptops, but all the other infrastructure elements

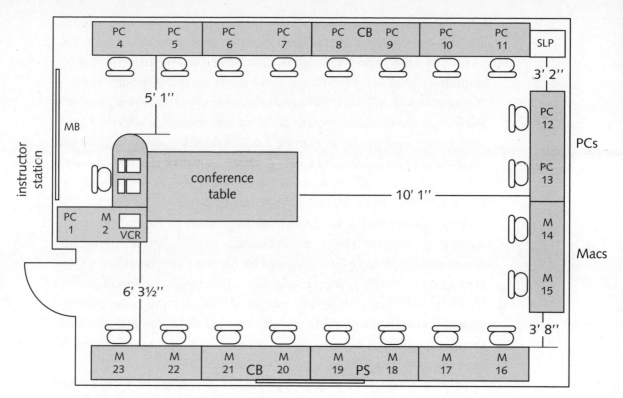

Figure 3.2 Computer Classroom Setup 2

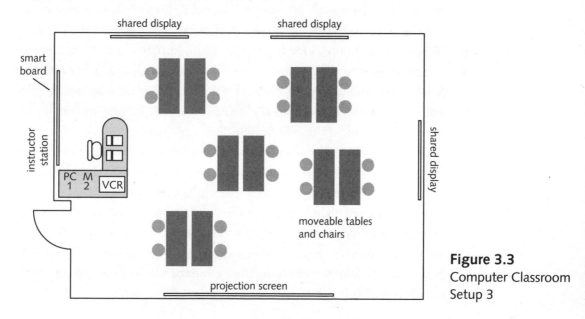

Figure 3.3
Computer Classroom
Setup 3

for collaborative writing are housed in the room, including wireless access, lots of power outlets, and large-sized shared screens mounted on the walls.

Closely linked with the design of physical space is the issue of time for computer access. Lab-focused computer access requires teachers (and, for that matter, writers) to plan around scheduled trips to the computer lab. But now, in increasing numbers of K–12 schools, cheaper, smaller, and more flexible computer systems have made it reasonable for districts to introduce computers, smart boards, and digital devices into regular classrooms where, when coupled with robust Internet bandwidth and wireless networking, they can become a routine part of instruction.

Two new trends now hold tremendous promise to expand classroom access: 1-to-1 computer programs and mobile devices. The 1-to-1 programs aim to make it possible for students to have a computer available to them at all times so that the computer—along with the tools and spaces accessible on the Internet—can be fully integrated into a learning environment. Typically associated with projects such as the Maine Laptop program from the Maine Learning Technology Initiative, these programs have thus far been found to lead to literacy gains (Warschauer, 2006).

In other cases, schools might not provide a fully configured laptop to each student, but might introduce netbooks or mobile devices for each student, combined with access to a smaller number of fully configured workstations for tasks not possible on the smaller devices. And, globally, projects such as Nicholas Negroponte's One Laptop Per Child Initiative and the increasing amount of freely available open source software—such as Mozilla's Firefox Web browser and the Open Office Suite sponsored by Sun Microsystems, as well as a variety of applications available from Source Forge—are moving us closer to truly ubiquitous and flexible digital environments.

Regardless of whether schools can, at this time, move toward fully realized computing environments, teachers and administrators should consider the impact of classroom design, spatial relationships, and access time as part of their instructional planning. Nancy Van Note Chism (2006), an educational space and learning researcher, has described several elements that should be part of any school's assessment of its learning environments. She suggests that spaces "harmonious with learning theory and the needs of current students" include several components, the first of which is flexibility.

Flexible spaces have moveable tables and chairs with shared displays, and foster different interaction modes (such as individual work, group work). Another component—a basic yet very important one—is comfort. In analyzing the lab floor plan in Figure 3.1, we noted the very limited space students have on the physical desktop. Spaces should allow learners of different sizes and shapes to be comfortable. Spaces should also be designed so that writers can have tools around them. Chism also notes the importance of spaces that engage the senses, arguing that "antiseptic environments consisting of white rectangles with overhead lights and bland tiled floors create a mood for the occupants of these spaces. Human beings yearn for color, natural and task-appropriate lighting, and interesting room shapes" (Chism, 2006, 2.7).

Perhaps the characteristic that trumps Chism's list is technology support. She argues that everyone—from people with seemingly endless digital creativity and know-how to people who are resistant to or uncomfortable with technology—needs support in multiple forms. This support might be another human being, who can experiment alongside the user or can help guide the user in a task. Or support might be linked to the tools in the room, such as a projector that can easily be connected to a laptop. Crafting spaces such as the ones we've described in this section is hard but important work, as is designing spaces with flexibility, comfort, sensory stimulation, and ready support as key affordances.

In some ways, we have come a long way from the experiences Childers describes—of lugging around twenty-seven-pound computers and mastering complicated keyboard commands. In other ways, however, we still have a long way to go before the physical space of many of our computer classrooms reflects a healthy ecology for digital writing.

COMPONENT TWO OF A HEALTHY DIGITAL ECOLOGY: ETHICAL, LEGAL, AND POLICY ENVIRONMENTS FOR DIGITAL WRITING

In addition to residing in a physical environment, digital writing exists in a mutlilayered environment shaped by ethical, legal, and policy concerns. For instance, before a teacher meets with his students in a computer lab they are asked to sign an acceptable use policy with specific rules for how the space and the machines in it can be used. Once the teacher and students go onto the Internet, they encounter an additional set of school-specific rules and policies that dictate how the larger network space can be used, which Web sites can be visited, and what content can be shared. Depending on the age of the students, these policies might have been developed in response to federal statutes that protect students' privacy and limit access to some content for our youngest students. As students begin to compose, they will face a second layer of ethical, legal, and policy issues. As writers use content found on the Internet, they must consider whether their use of material constitutes fair use or violates copyright. As they engage in social networking or responding to others, they must navigate privacy concerns and consider the boundaries of acceptable behavior within online communities. And as they research and write, they will need to understand the conventions of citation and the expectations for academic honesty with reference to a dizzying array of materials now available at their fingertips. All of these elements also shape a digital ecology.

Acceptable Use Policies

To help teachers and students successfully navigate the legal and ethical environment for digital writing, school districts and higher education institutions typically craft a set of AUPs that faculty and students must adhere to when they use school equipment, visit school labs, or go online. As part of a healthy digital ecology, effective AUPs balance a concern for the legal and ethical issues surrounding technology use and online access with a strong educational vision that seeks to support students as learners, creators, and developing digital citizens. Effective AUPs should be dynamic documents, shaped and reshaped in response to the rapidly evolving nature of online life and to our developing understanding of educational practice in online spaces.

Bud Hunt, instructional technologist for the St. Vrain Valley School District in northern Colorado and teacher-consultant with the Colorado State University Writing Project, has posted an acceptable use policy he crafted for the students at his school regarding their school-based blogs in his own wiki, budtheteacher.com. He admits, "I'd love for this document to be a proclamation that students should be able to say whatever they want, whenever they want, in a responsible manner, and be treated as if they were responsible adults. But I realize that is a bit idealistic—and also likely to get me shut down. . . . So, I need a practical policy that balances my concerns with the district's."

In crafting such a practical policy, Hunt (2005) discusses the context of student blogging (for example, who posts the blogs, how publicly accessible the blogs are) and offers his use policy for his blog readers to review and consider:

1. Students using blogs are expected to treat blogspaces as classroom spaces. Speech that is inappropriate for class is not appropriate for your blog. While we encourage you to engage in debate and conversation with other bloggers, we also expect that you will conduct yourself in a manner reflective of a representative of this school.

2. Students who violate the agreements here shall forfeit their right to school Internet access and will face other sanctions deemed appropriate by the administration.

3. Student blogs are to be a forum for student expression. However, they are first and foremost a tool for learning, and as such will sometimes be constrained by the various requirements and rules of classroom teachers. Students are welcome to post on any school-appropriate subject (this one might be hard to define. With blogging having such a personal emphasis, I wonder how we balance school and personal lives) at any time, outside of their classroom requirements.

Hunt's choice of a wiki to post his AUP is well tuned to the evolving nature of such policies as well as the need to invite broad collaboration in crafting, reviewing, and revising the AUP. And, as Renee Webster's experience illustrates, the specific provisions of AUPs can make a big difference in the environment of the classroom.

Yet there are a number of components that make crafting an AUP challenging. AUPs are always crafted with an eye toward some of the legal issues discussed in the previous chapter. For instance, privacy concerns, particularly for younger students, may affect access to the Internet or the publishing of student work. The provisions of the Children's Internet Protection Act of 2008 require schools and libraries where minors are present to (1) form policies that block or filter Internet access to pictures that are obscene, are child pornography, or are harmful to minors; (2) educate minors about inappropriate online behavior; (3) monitor online activities of minors; and (4) adopt a range of safety measures. Compliance with the Children's Internet Protection Act requires attention to curriculum and to infrastructure decisions, such as the use of filters.

These legal provisions have received widespread support; however, implementing them in a targeted way can be challenging. Filters designed to prevent access to obscene material can also prevent students from finding quality material as they conduct Internet research. Policies to protect student privacy might prevent them from publishing work in such a way that they can benefit from interaction with an audience. For this reason, the policies and procedures surrounding student Internet use need frequent review and revision so as to create a healthy—and safe—ecology for online work.

Copyright, Fair Use, and Creative Commons

Shaping a healthy digital ecology also requires attention to copyright. In the United States, there are federal laws that regulate the use of content— physical or digital. Writers are dealing with the law (whether they realize it or not) when they download an image from the Web to include in a slideshow presentation, for instance, or when they download an audio track to use in a digital essay.

The United States has a long history of taking people's intellectual property seriously. The Constitution of the United States notes that Congress has the power "to promote the progress of science and useful arts, by securing for limited times to authors and inventors the exclusive right to their respective writings and discoveries" (Article One, Section 8, Number 8). What this means is that if a writer comes up with a unique idea—for instance, a set of song lyrics and accompanying music, or an essay that explores a particular topic—and if that writer creates that idea in what the copyright offices of the U.S. government call a "fixed form of expression," the writer essentially "owns" that work for a set period of time. If others want to perform that song at a concert, or rerecord it for their own album, they must seek permission first. If others want to post the essay on a Web site, or publish it in a magazine, they have to seek permission first.

The U.S. government has also identified materials that cannot be owned. No one can own works that haven't been fixed in a tangible form of expression. So if, for instance, a dancer were to perform an interpretive dance that was not videorecorded, she could not "own" those particular dance moves. Individuals can't own a letter of the alphabet, or a number, or a system of measurement. A music note in and of itself cannot be owned, but music notes set in a unique format (such as an entire song) can be protected and owned.

This emphasis on ownership, however, is balanced by an interest in creativity and knowledge creation, and teachers who seek to provide students with access to digital materials they can use in composing have some resources at their disposal.

In U.S. law, a clause protects the open, free, and fair distribution of work for specific purposes: fair use. Fair use is addressed in Section 107 of the 1976 Copyright Act. Fair use allows for the use of a copyright-protected work for specific purposes: "criticism, comment, news reporting, teaching (including multiple copies for classroom use), scholarship, or research." These uses are generally not considered to be an infringement of copyright. What this means is that a teacher can make multiple copies of a copyright-protected essay to share with her students. An artist can manipulate a corporate logo to create a piece of cultural critique (although if the artist plans to sell his work, he may no longer be protected by fair use). A news reporter can include copyright-protected photographs or film footage in a news report.

Along with fair use, there are many resources that fall within the "public domain," as they were created before copyright law took effect, their copyright has expired, or they were intentionally left without copyright so that the public could use them. There are many online "public domain" resources where writers can access materials free from copyright control to use in their work (see www.publicdomainsherpa.com). As libraries, museums, and archives digitize and distribute their holdings online, the quantity of available copyright-free materials grows exponentially.

An excellent resource both for accessing materials and for helping students better understand how copyright works is Creative Commons (creativecommons.org), a form of copyright that was founded in 2001 by Lawrence Lessig and colleagues to provide an online space for people both to share materials and to tailor the licenses on those materials. For instance, a music teacher might write a song and want to invite others to use it, add to it, perform it, and teach with it, but might not want a company to be able to take the song and use it in an ad. Creative Commons allows that teacher to make the song available to his students and to protect it against commercial use. A science teacher might have prepared an excellent set of slideshows for teaching about volcanoes, and she wants to make it available to other teachers, but to keep those other teachers from changing the content. A Creative Commons license that does not allow derivative works ensures that the teacher can share her materials without worrying about others changing the content. As those who run and support Creative Commons tell users on their "What Is CC?" page, "We work to increase the amount of creativity (cultural, educational, and scientific content) in 'the commons'—the body of work that is available to the public for free and legal sharing, use, repurposing, and remixing." Creative Commons, by its very nature, encourages responsible use of others' works, as well as inherently supporting citation practices because composers of digital texts that rely on Creative Commons materials need to at least give attribution to the original authors of the works.

Writing teachers are not expected to be lawyers, but understanding some of the implications of copyright in digital space—especially when we ask students to create multimodal or multigenre work—is an important part of a healthy digital ecology. Fortunately, there are many resources to assist teachers in this area. The Center for Social Media at American University maintains a useful guide and set of instructional videos for media literacy educators. And media educators such as Renee Hobbs, law faculty such as Peter Jaszi, and more than 150 members of leading educational associations have worked together to create a significant resource available to writing teachers: the *Code of Best Practices in Fair Use for Media Literacy Education* (Center for Social Media, n.d.). This code was recently adopted by many organizations, including the National Council of Teachers of English.

The code is written as a guide that identifies principles representing "the media literacy education community's current consensus about acceptable practices for the fair use of copyrighted materials." The guide defines *media literacy* as "the capacity to access, analyze, evaluate, and communicate messages in a wide variety of forms." Reading and understanding this document can help teachers, administrators, and technology directors understand the broad rights that they and their students have in making "transformative" use of copyrighted materials.

Ethical Issues and Academic Honesty

Creating an environment where young writers can both access digital material for composing and understand the legal dimensions of their use is one important legal and ethical element of a healthy digital ecology. There are, of course, other ethical dimensions to digital composing and life online. One group that has sought to tease out the particular issues of ethics in online participation is the scholars and practitioners connected to the GoodPlay Project at Harvard University. The GoodPlay Project studied youth aged fifteen to twenty-five as they participated in online communities, such as social networking sites and gaming environments. Through a series of in-depth interviews and the examination of ethical dilemmas, GoodPlay outlined five critical areas of ethics in online environments (James, 2009):

- **Identity:** the ways people handle and perceive self-expression and identity exploration online
- **Privacy:** how, where, and with whom we share personal information online
- **Credibility:** how we establish trustworthiness of both people and information online, and establish our own personal credibility
- **Authorship and Ownership:** the ways we perceive intellectual property and practices, such as downloading or remixing content
- **Participation:** the meaning of responsible conduct and citizenship in online communities

These issues are not necessarily understood in the same way by young people and adults, an observation that was illustrated in a series of cross-generational dialogues on media ethics described in a report by GoodPlay Project, Global Kids, and Common Sense Media called *A Meeting of the*

Minds: Cross-Generational Dialogues on the Ethics of Digital Life (Global Kids, GoodPlay, and Common Sense, 2009). This work suggests that adults must be active partners with young people in surfacing and thinking about the ethical dimensions of digital writing and online life.

To help this partnership happen, Common Sense Media has created a curriculum to guide adults and youth in exploring these ethical dimensions of online life together (Common Sense Media, n.d.). Using a variety of case study materials and presenting activities for young people and the adults in their lives to do together, Common Sense Media's curriculum aims to empower young people to take responsibility for their own digital lives and help them develop the critical thinking skills that will allow them to navigate a changing digital ecology over time (see Web Resources). Deliberately crafted learning opportunities such as those created by Common Sense Media can help young people identify and reflect on the ethical dimensions of online life and bring that awareness into their work as writers and responders in online environments.

Although "authorship and ownership" make up only one of the ethical dimensions of online experience, academic institutions often focus on these particular issues, which attach to the concept of academic honesty and its negative corollary: plagiarism.

There are competing notions as to whether or not the Internet has encouraged plagiarism. Regardless of whether it has or has not, plagiarism has been a hot topic in school hallways, popular press accounts, and the blogs of myriad teachers. Interviewed on the *Frontline* special "Growing Up Online" (see Web Resources, Frontline's), social studies teacher Steve Maher sums up the feelings that many teachers experience related to academic honesty:

> Cheating is something that we talk about a lot, and it is something that we're concerned about, and it's mainly because of technology. There's no doubt that cheating is easier now. Since students have access to information, they have access to other essays; they have tons of sites out there willing to give them materials to cheat. . . . The question is how we react to that. And we can either react and say, OK, this is something that we have

to fight against; we have to make sure that they sit down and write an essay that they haven't had any background on, where they're not cheating at all. . . .

The other way to react to it is accept it as a reality and say that that's how the outside world works. . . . If a student is going to talk with a bunch of other students and network with them to exchange information to produce a paper, isn't that a skill that we want them to take to the workplace? (Maher, 2007)

Nonetheless, plagiarism can be a tricky concept. Maher's observation, for example, is very close to this real-world example:

A high school student intern working at a local nonprofit is developing a press release for an upcoming event. She accesses the networked archives for the office and finds several older press releases, and copies and pastes the general format and design from one older press release, along with the organization's contact information. She deletes the older contact info and inserts her own name as contact on the press release, then copies and pastes a portion of relevant text from another older press release and replaces information with details for the upcoming event. Her supervisor suggests some revisions, and eventually the press release is finalized and distributed. Another volunteer at the office, who does the organization's Web development work, accesses the networked archives for the press release and prepares it for Web publication, moving it from a word-processed document to a dynamic, Web-ready document. He again accesses the archives, this time looking for photographic content, and finds a photo from an earlier event. He adds this to the Web document, which is eventually reviewed by the office supervisor and published on the organization's website. (Maher, 2007)

Is this plagiarism? Or is this something else? Who is the "author" of the pieces the student intern pulled from? Of the press release that the student intern created? Who "owns" the photograph the Web developer selected to publish with the online version of the press release? Did either student "plagiarize" when using the existing press release as a template, copying and pasting chunks of text from the earlier press releases, or selecting a photo to reproduce from the organization's archives?

The focus on the single author and his or her solitary genius is, in academia, of the utmost importance in many areas, for example in literary studies. It is also evident in academia's focus on citation practices, which continually reconstitute the idea of original authorship. However, much digital writing is done in ways similar to how these writers prepared their press release—collaboratively, across time and space as well as across documents, and with what Lawrence Lessig (2008) has called "remixing" as a key practice for invention and composing—that is, writing by appropriation: taking bits, pieces, and ideas and compiling and remixing them in new and innovative ways. Sometimes these acts of appropriation, as the example above reveals, are done within an environment where this use is expected. These differences in expectation are part of the ecology for digital writing, and understanding them and making them explicit is an important teaching practice.

Indeed, citation practices represent an evolving and sophisticated skill set, as writers are required to consider what is "common knowledge" and what ideas "belong" to someone else. There are intellectual, cultural, and historical reasons to cite sources. Scholars and researchers who produce papers want to enhance their own credibility by showing that they've done appropriate research—that they've collected and sifted through the existing material available to them and cited sources appropriate to their fields or to their papers' specific subjects. Scholars also want to call attention to the work of others in order to show where their own work differs from or extends others' work. Researchers want to provide information to their audience, so that their readers can find and use the same sources of information they used. Web site authors create links to similar Web sites or to sources of information they relied upon as they crafted their Web sites in order to enhance their credibility and authority—to show not only that they're members of a digital community but also that they can be trusted. Considering citation in this way can make for a lively inquiry.

Some institutions have turned to plagiarism-detection software and Web sites like turnitin.com to identify student writing that may be "plagiarized." These technologies have inspired widespread adoption and ignited widespread discussion and concern. Plagiarism-detection software can be useful in identifying writing that has been copied outright. However, any teacher or administrator considering adopting such a program should be aware of a few considerations. Digital writing is complex, and new practices such as remixing are emerging as legitimate forms of composition. In digital composition, new citation practices are developing. The line between appropriate copying and plagiarism is a human line and cannot be patrolled by machine.

No one service or Web site is going to offer a magic fix that will instantly "cure" student plagiarism. Any approach to addressing plagiarism should be anchored by best practices and teaching moments. A few potential activities are included in the following box.

Activities for Situating Plagiarism in a Digital World

- Ask students to review the academic honesty or plagiarism policies of their school and prepare a one-page overview to guide their work.

- Engage students in research projects that ask them to define plagiarism and provide example cases and their repercussions.

- Create an in-class role play where students present and deliberate upon cases of potential plagiarism.

- Have students learn about the dimensions of plagiarism by doing it and reflecting on it. For instance, have students read an example piece that offers definitions of paraphrasing, patchwriting, and plagiarism, and ask them to select chunks of text, purposely creating their own examples of each type of plagiarism. Then have students explain what made these practices plagiarism as opposed to acceptable use.

- Ask students to review and evaluate the usefulness, correctness, and adequacy of online tutorials about plagiarism. If there's time, have students construct an online tutorial on plagiarism for their peers.

(continued)

- Give students a piece of digital media and have them trace the sources drawn upon or remixed—including recognizable influences, sampled work, quoted text, others' photographs or artwork, and so forth. Great examples include mashed or remixed movie trailers and the work of the musician Girl Talk (Gregg Michael Gillis).
- Have students compile an online resource for plagiarism examples and issues; consider publishing this online and adding to it each semester.

Privacy and protection, copyright and fair use, plagiarism, and citation are all part of the environment for digital writing, both out of school and in. A healthy digital writing ecology helps students learn to work in this environment, both by teaching about these areas and by supporting good practices.

COMPONENT THREE OF A HEALTHY DIGITAL ECOLOGY: ONLINE ENVIRONMENTS FOR DIGITAL WRITING

A final element of a healthy digital ecology relates to the online spaces where students compose, publish, and share their work. Much like physical spaces, online spaces support and invite particular types of interaction. Teachers can design activities and encourage practices in many ways within most online spaces, but much like trying to do group work in a lecture hall, it helps if the seats are not bolted to the floor.

The nature of "space" in online environments is, itself, complex—ranging from limited and focused interactions with online content or tools to broadly encompassing environments like virtual worlds or games, which provide settings in which individuals often use writing as one mode of participation among many. Local technology specialists and technology integration–focused networks like Classroom 2.0 (classroom20.com) can provide guidance on the ever-changing menu of commonly available tools and services. Most writing teachers are concerned with using these tools for three types of online activities, each of which can be done individually or collaboratively: accessing content for research and use in digital writing; accessing tools for composing and creating; and accessing spaces for publishing, sharing, and commenting on digital writing. Typically, tools for these activities also enable rich interaction within larger communities—whether they consist of one class, of several classes communicating across geographic boundaries, or of users of open Web sites available to the world.

An advantage of using commonly available tools and services for digital composing is that by doing so we introduce students to the range of options available to them outside of school, helping them manage their digital lives and become more productive across many domains. For students who are no longer minors and can take advantage of a range of opportunities not available to K–12 students, this is a particular advantage, as they learn about tools that will be potentially useful to them in the workforce or in college. For younger students, managing such environments often requires K–12 teachers who are willing to work with their districts on the modification of Internet filters that might be blocking access to such sites and who are able to think ahead about the student privacy practices as well as parental permissions necessary for students to publish and share their work. Nonetheless, these tools can enable powerful learning and composing experiences.

One disadvantage of many online tools and services available to consumers, though, is that they may not allow for the degree of customization that teachers might want. Teachers who are particularly interested in the design of their physical teaching spaces might feel stifled using online tools that do not allow user customization of the interface. Other issues include the presence of advertising, cumbersome procedures to manage class groups or student roles, and concerns about privacy and access for minors. Some services address these issues by creating education plans or services specifically for the K–12 education sector and packaging them together as offerings for schools, but these often come with their own particular set of advantages and disadvantages.

Increasingly, educators with experience in teaching digital writing are trying to get beyond the inadequacies of some digital tools and services by creating their own spaces to support a strong ecology for teaching digital writing. Many focus their efforts on publishing student work online; others are working to create networked environments for students to interact and share with each other.

Creating an Online Environment: Youth Voices

High school teachers Paul Allison, of the New York City Writing Project, and Chris Sloan, of the Wasatch Range Writing Project, have been teaching digital writing for many years. Over the course of their careers, as tools and environments have changed, they have become increasingly interested in creating and managing interactive environments that support both young writers and their teachers. Working together with networks of other teachers, they have created curricula and online spaces for students to share and comment on podcasts, to blog together, and to create and post videos. These early efforts led them to decide to create a larger online environment for their teaching called Youth Voices (youthvoices.net).

Youth Voices is a safe social network where teachers' collaborative planning frames flexible activities that invite quality writing and image production from students. Allison and Sloan (along with a number of other colleagues) began Youth Voices with the support of a minigrant from the National Writing Project in 2005. It has now blossomed into an online community of youth writers, as well as a small network of teachers dedicated to keeping their writers engaged, safe, and responding productively to the work of others.

For Allison, elements of effective writing instruction—such as writing for real audiences and developing a strong voice—can be amplified in networked spaces. "What happens in blogging and in podcasting is these things that can seem almost imaginary to students become real," states Allison, now teaching at the East-West School of International Studies in Flushing, New York. "You're not just writing to an imaginary audience. . . . My students know that they are writing to other kids who have been 'friended' in some way, and are following [them] so that there is a real audience that you are writing for." By working together to pursue topics of similar interest, students actually build off one another's research and contribute useful information to the Youth Voices community, helping others make connections to resources that they might not have found on their own.

For Sloan, a teacher at Judge Memorial Catholic High School in Salt Lake City, Utah, these connections are critical. For instance, when thinking about digital writing, he aims to have students write more focused pieces. "As we read on the Internet, we don't give things much time," Sloan believes.

"Teaching them how to write differently for paper and how to write differently for online stuff is something that I am starting to realize [the importance of] now—how to storyboard for video, and how to do that for audio, too, is different." As we think about how readers (or listeners and viewers) take in digital texts, there are moments where talking about purpose, audience, and media all come into play, and helping students understand different writing contexts matters.

As Allison and Sloan reflect on how digital writing has developed in their classrooms, they point to many elements of a strong ecology. Both assert that responsible use of copyrighted materials has been a cornerstone of their collaboration. Students incorporate a variety of images, audio, video, and text into their blogging (as well as creating some of their own), and Allison and Sloan make sure that students use materials under a Creative Commons copyright. This is one of the community values that students learn through being a part of Youth Voices.

Sloan and Allison also point to the importance of ongoing, sustained writing as a practice distinct from occasional trips to a computer lab or occasional Internet searches. Sloan notes that digital writing "opens up the black box of revision." Posting their writing on the Youth Voices network forces it to be archived and searchable, allowing students to revisit their own—and others'—work in order to develop and refine ideas for future writing. If students make mistakes, then the teachers look at it as an experience for growth. Also, according to Allison, students learn to be responsible contributors to the network. Allison, Sloan, and other teachers associated with Youth Voices are proactive participants in managing and contributing to the network. In other words, students do not act as solitary authors; they learn how to become digital writers participating in a community.

Allison sums up their philosophy like this: "You recognize that what you are doing [allowing students to participate in a social network] is a chance, but you show the student work and say that there is value in taking this chance, and if something goes wrong, we'll manage it." The network of teachers constantly monitor student work and support each other's teaching. For everyone involved, this recursive process of posting, reading, and writing anew contributes to their students' growth as writers, as well as to the writing workshop community in and across their classrooms.

Along with teacher Susan Ettenheim, Allison hosts a weekly Webcast, *Teachers Teaching Teachers*, in which he and his colleagues discuss digital writing, the design of Youth Voices, and useful tools that might be incorporated into the community. These are then archived and available as podcasts. They also maintain an active, collaborative space for faculty and youth leaders within Youth Voices to support the collaborative planning that allows the space to function for them as a centerpiece in their curricula. Together these educators have become stewards of their digital ecology, a stance that provides them with important opportunities for teaching and learning digital writing.

TOWARD STEWARDSHIP: SUSTAINING HEALTHY DIGITAL ECOLOGIES

This chapter has addressed some of the crucial aspects of a healthy digital ecology: physical space and layout appropriate to writing pedagogy; attention to policy-related and legal issues that affect writing-related work in digital spaces; and the design of online spaces. These issues—and all other issues related to a healthy digital ecology, including the others listed at the start of the chapter—require technology stewardship. Dickie Selfe, author of *Sustainable Computer Environments* (2005), uses the expression "technology activist" to identify individuals "willing to productively influence and shape the technological systems around them" (xiii). In the book, Selfe describes cultures of support that

- Encourage teachers to use computers [and] help them actively shape computer environments in their K–college institutions
- Foster methods for sustaining professional development efforts
- Allow for collaboration with a range of individuals to design and operate technology-rich labs, classrooms, and virtual systems
- Engage students and administrators, as well as faculty and staff, in assessing the success of computer-supported communication
- Develop a core of student support staff

At present, classroom teachers and university professors are rarely involved with many of the items on this list. Equipment is purchased and installed, Internet filters activated, acceptable use policies developed or revised, and contracts for online tools and services proffered. At present, most teachers would say they do not have the expertise, nor are they provided with the time and training, to become involved in core decisions about their digital ecologies. Those who do—like Renee Webster, Paul Allison, and Chris Sloan—might currently be considered "activists," teachers who have taken a stance toward digital writing that, at the very least, moves beyond merely accepting the typical conceptions of how technology is used in schools.

In the future, we imagine this will change. Future generations of teachers and administrators might come to the profession with strong experience— and preferences—in digital environments. More flexible and scalable technology solutions will make teacher collaborations more reasonable to institutional administrators. Teachers of digital writing might more generally come to view the digital ecology as central to the teaching and learning experiences they want to foster.

Therefore, rather than *activist,* we use the expression *steward.* Stewardship is an activity integral to sustainability. As stewards, teachers might well address the five activities that Selfe lists, and do so in a way that is sensitive to the impact on student learning, and that fosters their own ability to work together and to create and share technology-rich lesson plans, assignments, and activities. A healthy digital writing ecology is nurtured when teachers act as stewards, and as they engage their colleagues, administrators, and students in ongoing discussions about the many issues related to physical space, about policy implications, and about responsible use of technologies. In so doing, they create new opportunities for teaching and learning, ones that many professional organizations and policy groups have called for in terms of standards and assessments for digital writing.

chapter FOUR

Standards and Assessment for Digital Writing

For classroom teachers in the United States, there is no escaping the fact that the proliferation of new digital tools is happening concurrently with a strong national and state accountability movement that emphasizes standards and assessment as the centerpiece for educational reform. For many teachers, this presents a Janus-like challenge: they must look forward to the emergent skills and capacities their students will need in the world after graduation while simultaneously helping students meet the goals and benchmarks that mean they actually *will* graduate. Professional associations such as the National Council of Teachers of English (NCTE), the International Reading Association (IRA), and numerous content-area organizations have recognized this challenge and are advocating for revised standards that take account of new media studies and multimodal literacy. But the work of actually developing those standards as part of state and local policy—let alone the task of developing assessments in relation to those standards—still lies before us.

Teachers who stress digital writing, such as NWP teacher-consultants Kevin Hodgson and Dave Boardman, are hopeful that new standards and assessments for digital writing will develop in a direction that can connect closely with their efforts to create a positive environment for digital writers. Understanding the *what* and *how* of digital writing should inform new standards and approaches to assessment. Standards and assessments, in turn, would then support strong learning environments and encourage student growth. But balancing the *what* and *how* in an area marked by evolving forms of discourse and rapid technological change will require careful consideration and thoughtful planning. Will digital writing be seen as part of a larger set of technology standards? Will technology use be seen as an essential part of writing standards? Or both?

Hodgson, a sixth-grade teacher at William E. Norris Elementary School in Massachusetts and a teacher-consultant with the Western Massachusetts Writing Project, tries to achieve such a balance in his classroom, making sure that students have a chance to learn the *how* of specific technology skills while understanding that their use is for communicating and creating. From their individual blogs and podcasts to group-created wiki pages, from digital stories to claymation videos, Hodgson's students engage in the composing process every day. "In general I want my students to see themselves as writers, real writers," Hodgson says, "so, when I think about how I am using technology, I really try to emphasize with them that the things we are doing are helping them become real, published writers."

Hodgson takes a three-pronged approach to structuring his curriculum. First, he builds in technology skills across the school year rather than all at once for a particular project. "If you throw everything at them at once," he believes, "then a lot of the kids will just be overwhelmed with the technical aspect of it, and they won't get enough out of the writing, publishing, and creating aspects of it." Second, he provides dedicated time and space to learn the technology skills. Thus students begin to develop particular skills—such as embedding an image or recording their voices—and those skills become second nature by the time the students get to bigger projects. Third, Hodgson intentionally and routinely engages students in purposeful talk about writing in relation to the technology in use, emphasizing the rhetorical choices students make across different modes, and raising questions of design. For instance, when creating enhanced podcasts of a persuasive essay, he suggests that "as the writer, you are controlling what you want the reader to see. So that kind of platform can really change how you persuade somebody. When you are editing, and you have images, you may think about having fewer words and how you balance what you are saying as opposed to what you are showing." Through this ongoing discussion of the rhetorical choices that digital writers make, and the observation of their effects, students begin to understand better how to assess their work as digital writers. This ongoing self-assessment can draw on and carry forward to their work in digital environments outside his classroom as well.

Dave Boardman, a teacher-consultant with the Maine Writing Project and an English teacher at Messalonskee High School in Oakland, Maine, agrees that this self-assessment is the foundation for meaningful assessment in the classroom. Like Hodgson, Boardman is careful to name the differences that make specific types of digital writing work: "Rather than the traditional style of students' writing more and more and trying to develop length, I think that a lot of times the focus in [digital] composing has been on sound, the ability to engage an audience right away, and the recognition that there will be an audience for this work."

Sometimes this is best done in only a few words, instead of a lengthy essay. In fact, one digital writing assignment that Boardman uses is for students to boil down a five-hundred-word story into one hundred words, supplementing their narration with images to compose a digital story. Nonetheless, Boardman argues, "To write well, students need to write a lot. And they need to be writing steadily in different ways—including academic essays and papers." In Boardman's classroom, students create films and digital stories, but they also engage in more traditional forms of writing—such as composing structured essays—because he knows that future teachers, as well as tests such as the SAT, will require students to produce such essays.

In many cases, the ability to compare what works for different audiences across different media, modes, and tools presents an ideal opportunity for literacy learning. Most school-based educators would note, however, that only a limited range of literacy products carry the weight of accountability requirements. As Anne Herrington and Charles Moran (2009) observe in

Teaching the New Writing: Technology, Change, and Assessment in the 21st-Century Classroom:

> At the same time that new forms of writing—and thus literacy—are emerging in our culture and in our classrooms, forces of assessment and standardization exert a counter-pressure, asking us to prepare students to produce conventional, formulaic print texts in scripted ways. . . . So it is that technology seems to be leading us forward to new forms of writing, but, as used by standardized testing programs, backward to the five-paragraph theme. (2)

Furthermore, the skills and capacities essential to new digital literacies can be directly at odds with norms and expectations that undergird most assessment programs. Michele Knobel and Colin Lankshear (2007) have described this as a conflict of "mind-sets." For Knobel and Lankshear, new literacies do not just include new technologies, but also new "ethos stuff":

> When we say that new literacies involve different "*ethos* stuff" from that which is typically associated with conventional literacies, we mean that new literacies are more "participatory," "collaborative", and "distributed" in nature than conventional literacies. That is, they are less "published," "individuated," and "author-centric" than conventional literacies. (9)

The "ethos stuff" described here, which holds for many areas of digital writing where the emphasis on expanded collaboration is a central value, stands in contrast to standards and assessments that emphasize individual students' being tested on their stand-alone accomplishments. How, then, can we best situate technological competencies and emerging forms of literacy within the landscape of state and national standards and assessments? And how can we support that delicate balance between fostering growth in new literacies and pursuing an interest in larger technology competencies?

THE DOUBLE HELIX OF STANDARDS IN WRITING AND IN TECHNOLOGY

This chapter looks at places where technology content standards and writing content standards are beginning to align with one another, and suggests some principles for assessing student digital writing. This chapter also includes case studies of effective practices in assessment, and considers how assessment can be used effectively to understand student progress and instructional needs in digital writing practices.

Standards for technology or technology literacy are relatively new. The National Assessment of Educational Progress (NAEP), for example, only began developing frameworks for technology literacy in 2008, with a first assessment to be conducted in 2012. These newer standards, then, must enter into a field already crowded with standards and assessments for other areas of the curriculum, such as writing. Given this history, technology content standards and writing content standards more often run parallel to one another than intersect. Most current writing content standards stand alone and focus exclusively on written text; and many technology standards pay little attention to achievement in digital writing though they may stress that students should be familiar with technology tools. Ideally, standards for technology and for digital writing would be intertwined: a double helix of writing and technology. As Elyse Eidman-Aadahl argued at the "Digital Is . . ." Convening (2009):

> This is a critical issue for teachers of writing right now. In many cases, groups have developed standards projects from a technology integration and use perspective that require students to demonstrate their technical abilities in digital environments. Most of what students will be doing in those digital environments will be reading, writing, creating, and responding, but the standards won't be framed in such a way that teachers will be able to see the threads of literacy development in these environments. On the other hand, to just look at the literacy outcomes without understanding the mediated practices students engage in across all modes, and the impact of those practices on what it means to read, write, create, and respond, is also insufficient.

Teaching writing is about more than just the technical act of saving a document on a computer, and it is certainly about more than just being able to write in the sense that we put words down in a certain order. Decades of composition research have shown us that literacy is a situated act, and technologies add another layer to the idea of what it means to "be literate." As the next section elaborates in more detail, there are a number of standards documents that focus on technologies and their use, a number that focus on literacy and language arts, and a number that focus on the dispositions of a twenty-first-century learner. As we think about what it means to be a digital writer, and to teach digital writing, our question then shifts from specific objectives (composing in a word processor, crafting a thesis statement) into something broader about what it means to be literate in a digital world. Thus, we ask, how do these distinct sets of standards relate and what implications do they have for digital writing practices?

A Brief Look at Technology Standards

Whether called "twenty-first-century skills," "digital literacies," or "technology expectations," emerging technology standards present educators with an ever-expanding list of what students should know and be able to do with computers and the read/write Web. Even as few as five years ago, typical instruction and expectations for computer literacy focused mostly on computer operations, such as the ability to create and save a file, change fonts and adjust other document formatting features, and perhaps share a document via e-mail or a networked storage device. More recently, however, some state curriculum documents and assessments have moved toward the inclusion of multimodal composition, and most emphasize technology development and skill built over time and across experiences. Not all of the technology standards relate specifically to writing; in fact, many transcend specific subject areas. Writing instruction thus does not carry the entire burden of students' development with technology, but insofar as students write across the curriculum and in service of the disciplines, it can be positioned to play a significant part.

One of the earliest efforts to clarify technology standards is provided by the Mid-continent Research for Education and Learning (McREL). The McREL standards owe their genesis to *Technology for All Americans: A*

Rationale and Structure for the Study of Technology, a 1996 report from the International Technology Education Association (ITEA). Four years later, ITEA published *Standards for Technological Literacy: Content for the Study of Technology* (2000) as a way to define "what students should know and be able to do in order to be technologically literate" (vii). These twenty standards cover the nature of technology, technology and society, abilities needed in a technological world, and understanding the designed world. Also in 2000—and again in 2007—the International Society for Technology in Education (ISTE) published *National Educational Technology Standards for Students,* which covers ten performance indicators for various grades, also arrayed in several broad categories.

Drawing on these documents as well as documents prepared for subject-matter standards, McREL (2009) crafted umbrella technology standards, which suggest that a well-prepared student

1. Knows the characteristics and uses of computer hardware and operating systems.

2. Knows the characteristics and uses of computer software programs.

3. Understands the relationships among science, technology, society, and the individual.

4. Understands the nature of technological design.

5. Understands the nature and operation of systems.

6. Understands the nature and uses of different forms of technology.

Even since 2000, however, what students would need to know and understand to meet these standards has been rapidly changing. Focusing on writing, for example, an arts and communication technology benchmark for high school students is that each student "knows techniques used to publish printed media (e.g., techniques for various journalistic products such as advertisements, newspapers, and magazines; components of publication including reporting, writing, headlines, captions, and photography)." This important benchmark points to an area of media that is being profoundly affected by the use of technologies—students use graphic-design and page-layout software to produce newspapers and magazines, for instance, and rely on digital databases to obtain materials for their journalistic work. Furthermore, in addressing print journalism, the McREL standards point to an area of production undergoing historic transformation, one which will never be the same owing to the introduction of networked communications, the shift from print to digital publication, and the rise of "citizen journalism" in digital space. In five to ten years we will still likely want students to know and understand the techniques of print journalism, but we will also want them to understand how these techniques have evolved and what has caused such dramatic changes.

More recent standards documents attempt to mitigate this problem— that is, how to address the constantly changing technological landscape— in a variety of ways. The state of Michigan, for example, has shaped content standards that define *technology literacy* as "the ability to responsibly use appropriate technology to communicate, solve problems, and access, manage, integrate, evaluate, and create information to improve learning in all subject areas and to acquire lifelong knowledge and skills in the 21st century." It is significant that across the Michigan standards, technology use is encouraged in ways that appropriately complement and extend the curriculum. That is, technology is not situated as an exclusive thing or as justifying a separate set of standards, but instead is embedded within goals across the content areas.

For instance, in terms of the language arts, Michigan's curriculum framework identifies a literate individual as someone who

- Communicates skillfully and effectively through printed, visual, auditory, and technological media in the home, school, community, and workplace

- Thinks analytically and creatively about important themes, concepts, and ideas

- Uses the English language arts to identify and solve problems

- Uses the English language arts to understand and appreciate the commonalities and differences within social, cultural, and linguistic communities

- Understands and appreciates the aesthetic elements of oral, visual, and written texts

- Uses the English language arts to develop insights about human experiences
- Uses the English language arts to develop the characteristics of lifelong learners and workers, such as curiosity, persistence, flexibility, and reflection
- Connects knowledge from all curriculum areas to enhance understanding of the world

These flexible standards resonate with the ways in which more recent technological change has occurred. Multimedia authoring tools—such as audio- and video-editing software and photo-management tools—have become easier to use, and are also common on nearly every personal computer. Today, the processes of multimodal composing and the products of digital writing can be engaged, created, and shared using a personal computer. The standards, which address perennial purposes of communication and meaning making, are, in some ways, better able to address the many technological changes that continue to occur. That is, rather than codifying specific technology skills, standards such as these allow for a more liberal interpretation of how and why to employ digital writing tools in the service of content-area curriculum goals.

In the example standards included thus far, we see proponents of twenty-first-century skills looking for a larger framework to encapsulate them. One such framework is offered by the International Society for Technology in Education's publication *Digital Citizenship in Schools* (Ribble and Bailey, 2007). Mike Ribble and Gerald Bailey assert, "As educators, we must prepare students to live in a world without physical boundaries and help them learn how to work with others, virtual or otherwise. 'Citizenship' in this sense takes on a new meaning beyond our normal understanding of geographic nations, states, and communities. Indeed, this new citizenship is global in nature. . . . A common framework, such as digital citizenship, provides us all with a starting point for understanding each other" (12). Ribble and Bailey go on to present nine elements of digital citizenship:

1. **Digital Access:** full electronic participation in society
2. **Digital Communication:** electronic exchange of information

3. **Digital Literacy:** the capability to use digital technology and knowing when and how to use it

4. **Digital Etiquette:** standards of conduct expected by other digital technology users

5. **Digital Commerce:** the buying and selling of goods online

6. **Digital Law:** the legal rights and restrictions governing technology use

7. **Digital Rights and Responsibilities:** the privileges and freedoms extended to all digital technology users, and the behavioral expectations that come with them

8. **Digital Health and Wellness:** the elements of physical and psychological well-being related to technology use

9. **Digital Security:** the precautions all technology users must take to guarantee their personal safety and the security of their networks

Although two elements of digital citizenship relate directly to digital writing—communication and literacy—it is easy to see that enabling students to participate in digital worlds as creators and communicators will eventually touch on most of the nine elements.

Indeed, despite the diversity of frameworks and the need for a common language, there is a convergence of spirit in the many documents purporting to identify twenty-first-century skills. This spirit—which points to student engagement, creativity, collaboration, and participation in society through technology—resonates with the spirit of recent work in the teaching of writing that encourages an approach to writing instruction in which students write for real purposes in an atmosphere of choice and responsibility, where teacher-to-student and student-to-student conferring and collaboration happens frequently, and where students publish their work to an audience beyond the classroom.

This spirit, which stresses participation in the larger social processes that will define the twenty-first century, is the approach developed by the Partnership for 21st Century Skills (P21), an advocacy group that brings together the business community, education leaders, and policymakers to provide a powerful model of twenty-first-century education. P21 has worked to create an integrated set of standards for core subjects, twenty-first-century skills, and educational policy. Broadly conceived as a "roadmap," the P21 standards link expectations for curriculum and student performance to political processes in which states agree to adopt the P21 roadmap. The broad and integrative approach that seeks to blend technology skills with core curriculum standards aims to create a single umbrella for the concept of twenty-first-century skills that can be used to enlist states in organizing around a broad change process for teaching, standards, and assessments in public education.

According to Will Banks, assistant professor of English at East Carolina University and co-director of the Tar River Writing Project, this is a sensible approach. "What these [digital writing] technologies do is create a set of dispositions, habits of mind, ways of being in the world, ways of collaborating, ways of working together, ways of linking information, ways of building knowledge," he explains. "Those are the things that are going to be really important in the careers and the futures of our students." Standards, guidelines, and skills statements that position themselves under the broad heading of "twenty-first-century skills" seem to point to a shared understanding about what it means to move from the types of learning that valued memorization and basic application to those that are commonly defined as "digital literacies."

Twenty-First-Century Skills: Convergences Across Documents

Below we provide a collection of words and phrases that we feel convey the integrated, rich, and complex approaches to literacy and technology as described above. These words and phrases are common in a number of standards documents that relate, directly or indirectly, to digital writing. Documents consulted include the "NCTE Framework for 21st Century Curriculum and Assessment" (National Council of Teachers of English, 2008); the Partnership for 21st Century Skills' "21st Century Skills Map" (n.d.); the Center for Media Literacy's "Literacy for the 21st Century: An Overview & Orientation Guide to Media Literacy Education" (2008); ISTE's National Educational Technology Standards for Students (2007); and the collaboratively authored "Code of Best Practices in Fair Use for Media Literacy Education" (Center for Social Media, n.d.). This collection of standards is not exhaustive, nor is this list alone meant to be a comprehensive comparison of the documents and their content. Instead, it is intended to be a concise summary of key words that teachers, administrators, policy-makers, business leaders, and researchers have introduced into the discourse surrounding twenty-first-century education in general and digital writing in particular. We have left out references to "traditional" and still very much valued language arts activities (reading, writing, listening, speaking, viewing, and visually representing), and focused instead on the habits of mind and activities in which students are expected to engage as digital writers.

Condensed List of Traits and Actions

- **Creativity and Originality**
  - Create
  - Design
  - Develop
  - Express
  - Innovate
  - Invent
  - Produce
- **Collaboration**
  - Cocreate
  - Collaborate
  - Compromise
  - Contribute
  - Give feedback
  - Receive feedback
  - Share
- **Management and Leadership**
  - Implement
  - Initiate
  - Manage
  - Lead
  - Plan
  - Prioritize
  - Organize

- **Evaluation and Decision Making**
  - Critique
  - Evaluate
  - Influence
  - Set criteria
  - Choose
  - Decide
  - Impact
- **Diversity**
  - Cross-cultural understanding
  - Diverse perspectives
  - Globalization
  - Interdisciplinary
- **Articulation**
  - Articulate
  - Clarify
  - Define
  - Form
  - Frame
  - Select
- **Critical Thinking and Problem Solving**
  - Expand
  - Forecast

- Identify fallacies, key concepts, solutions, trends
- Interpret
- Reason
- **Observation and Inquiry**
  - Ask
  - Examine
  - Explore
  - Inquire
  - Investigate
  - Observe
  - Question
  - Research
- **Communication in Rhetorical Contexts**
  - Audience
  - Authorship
  - Perception
  - Point of view
  - Purpose
  - Communicate
  - Connect
  - Interact
- **Knowledge Making**
  - Apply
  - Construct
  - Demonstrate
  - Discover
  - Emulate
  - Incorporate
  - Integrate
  - Model
  - Synthesize
  - Analyze
  - Deconstruct
- Examine
- Process
- **Information Literacy**
  - Determine significance
  - Evaluate
  - Gather
  - Locate
  - Utilize
- **Personal Habits of Mind**
  - Accountable
  - Accurate
  - Adaptable
  - Efficient
  - Effective
  - Flexible
  - Gaining expertise
  - Metacognition
  - Quality of work
  - Responsive
  - Self-evaluation
  - Understanding complexity
  - Valuing diversity
- **Remix Culture**
  - Amplify
  - Attribute
  - Circulate
  - Distribute
  - Disseminate
  - Engage
  - Ethical use
  - Modify
  - Participate
  - Publish
  - Remix
  - Repurpose

- Re-present
- Share
- Stimulate
- Transform
- **Technology Knowledge and Issues**
  - Applications
  - Digital media environments
  - Systems
- **Digital Citizenship**
  - Active
  - Creative Commons
  - Copyright
  - Democratic process
  - Fair use
  - Participant
  - Lifelong learner

Given the many components of what it means, then, to be "digitally literate" or a "twenty-first-century learner," we see that teaching and learning digital writing can be construed less as a particular set of curricular goals and more as a set of dispositions toward how we receive and express ourselves through language.

A Brief Look at Standards and Assessments Specific to Digital Writing

When attention turns specifically to digital writing, some standards documents have chosen to layer digital writing onto other valued competencies in literacy. For example, in 2006 the Michigan Department of Education released their English Language Arts High School Content Expectations (HSCEs), which included among their ninety standards the following examples that focus on the tools and techniques of digital writing (emphases added):

- CE 1.2.3 Write, speak, and create artistic representations to express personal experience and perspective (e.g., personal narrative, poetry, imaginative writing, slam poetry, **blogs, Web pages**). (5)

- CE 1.3.9 Use the formal, stylistic, content, and mechanical conventions of a variety of genres in speaking, writing, and **multimedia presentations**. (6)

- CE 1.4.2 Develop a system for gathering, organizing, paraphrasing, and summarizing information; select, evaluate, synthesize, and use multiple primary and secondary (print and **electronic**) resources. (7)

- CE 1.5.4 Use technology tools (e.g., **word processing, presentation and multimedia software**) to produce polished written and **multimedia** work (e.g., literary and expository works, proposals, business presentations, advertisements).

- CE 2.1.2 Make supported inferences and draw conclusions based on informational print and **multimedia** features (e.g., prefaces, appendices, marginal notes, **illustrations**, bibliographies, author's pages, footnotes, **diagrams, tables, charts, maps, timelines, graphs, and other visual and special effects**) and explain how authors and speakers use them to infer the organization of text and enhance understanding, convey meaning, and inspire or mislead audiences.

- CE 2.2.2 Examine the ways in which prior knowledge and personal experience affect the understanding of written, spoken, or **multimedia** text.

- CE 3.4.4 Understand how the **commercial and political purposes** of producers and publishers influence not only the nature of advertisements and the selection of media content, but the slant of news articles in **newspapers, magazines, and the visual media**.

Many other standards documents could be revised in similar ways to include some aspect of digital writing in English language arts or elsewhere in the curriculum. Indeed, digital writing—because it involves text, image, audio, and video—could be introduced in all content areas. Understanding how, for instance, to create a chart with a spreadsheet program is just as much about the numbers themselves, perhaps learned in math and science, as it is about designing a chart that represents the data in an ethically and aesthetically pleasing manner. In addition, the ways in which students respond through classroom discussion and writing have been adapted for use with blogs, discussion forums, and other virtual worlds (Webb and Rozema, 2008).

In the Michigan standards and in others, we see developments occurring along two parallel lines: first, twenty-first-century skills, and second, writing standards, framed by a growing attention to digital composition as a new layer to consider in addition to more traditional content. These are positive changes in how we approach and assess writing. Both the developments in the standards themselves and the developments in how we focus attention on practices of digital writing help teachers see avenues for introducing new forms of writing into their classrooms.

So what is to be gained in pursuing the integration of these new forms of writing—as exemplified by the work of teachers like Kevin Hodgson and Dave Boardman—which makes for a double helix of technology standards and writing standards? We would assert that through their integration, we can more fully understand and address the "ethos stuff," to reference Knobel and Lankshear, that accompanies the "technical stuff." For example, Eve Bearne (2009), drawing on experiences and lessons learned through the More Than Words work in the United Kingdom, proposes a scheme for multimodal writing. Bearne explains that multimodal writing is marked by the increasing ability to

1. Decide on mode and content for specific purpose(s) and audience(s)
   - Choose which mode(s) will best communicate meaning for specific purposes
   - Use perspective, colour, sound, and language to engage and hold a reader's/viewer's attention
   - Select appropriate content to express personal intentions, ideas, and opinions
   - Adapt, synthesise, and shape content to suit personal intentions in communication
2. Structure texts
   - Pay conscious attention to design and layout of texts, use structural devices (pages, sections, frames, paragraphs, blocks of text screens, sound sequences) to organize texts
   - Integrate and balance modes for design purposes
   - Structure longer texts with visual, verbal, and sound cohesive devices
   - Use background detail to create mood and setting
3. Use technical features for effect
   - Handle technical aspects and conventions of different kinds of multimodal texts, including line, colour, perspective, sound, camera angles, movement, gesture, facial expression, and language

- Choose language, punctuation, font, typography, and presentational techniques to create effects and clarify meaning
- Choose and use a variety of sentence structures for specific purposes
4. Reflect
   - Explain choices of mode(s) and expressive devices including words
   - Improve own composition or performance, reshaping, redesigning, and redrafting for purpose and readers'/viewers' needs
   - Comment on the success of a composition in fulfilling the design aims
   - Comment on the relative merits of teamwork and individual contribution for a specific project. (21)

Bearne notes that this "suggested framework makes it possible to describe the development of multimodal text makers from: *a multimodal text maker in the early stages* through to being *an increasingly assured multimodal text maker*, then becoming *a more experienced and often independent multimodal text maker*. The descriptors offer teachers a starting point from which they may develop a vocabulary to talk about multimodal texts, since establishing a metalanguage is an essential part of creating possibilities for assessment which value all elements of multimodality" (21).

Thus, the act of writing has changed with the introduction of digital tools and standards that ask for collaboration, creativity, and effective design. Yet, in many ways, writing is the same as it ever was—a task that requires writers to examine the rhetorical context and craft messages suitable for the intended audience. And when we examine this task within the context of twenty-first-century skills, digital writing tools, and frameworks for approaching multimedia, we can better articulate what is important about digital writing—the immeasurable possibilities for who, how, and why we compose texts.

FOCUSING ON ASSESSMENT: WHAT ABOUT THE WRITING ITSELF?

The metalanguage for talking about purposeful digital writing described in the standards provides an essential bridge to thinking about assessments. Smart assessment honors the fact that students can learn to *improve* their work as digital writers; blogging or filmmaking, for example, are not just activities students can do, they are also practices they can get better at.

Quality in digital writing, as in all writing, can be assessed in various ways: Does the piece achieve its intended purpose? Does it resonate with an audience? Does it meet various accepted standards of performance for products of its type? One of the advantages of digital tools and environments is how they extend the writer's capacity to reach a wide audience, including audience members quite distant from the classroom itself. And those audience members will often be able to respond to or act upon a piece, potentially providing feedback as to whether it achieved its purpose. This "response-centered" approach to assessment focuses on helping students inquire into and analyze audience response, and is well suited to the kinds of collaborative classroom processes that leverage new media. Furthermore, since audience reception is at the core of writing, an assessment culture that values audience will support the development of vital rhetorical skills.

More challenging, however, is pinpointing accepted standards of performance. In a field marked by rapid change in the types and discourses of digital writing, some elements of accepted standards of performance are being reinvented. Current forms of large-scale assessment in writing, as well as much classroom assessment, depend on rubrics and assessment tools that specify and value attributes of effective writing. In most cases, these attributes will easily transfer to many forms of digital writing. In other cases, they may work at cross-purposes. To the degree that assessment scales, such as rubrics, are sensitive to audience, purpose, and diversity in form, they will be easily adapted. Those, however, that reward specific, perhaps formulaic, elements of form will be counterproductive. Critics of large-scale standardized assessments in writing, such as Hillocks (2002) and Wilson (2006), have documented how high-stakes assessments can have the effect of narrowing curricula and inhibiting high-quality writing instruction. At best formulaic and at worst completely contrived, the practice of writing responses for these types of tests has distorted the original intent of the writing process approach.

Thus, when considering the types of skills and practices that digital writing demands, considering what is assessed—as well as how it is assessed—becomes a pressing task. Digital writing will place differing emphases on common skills (brainstorming, drafting, and revising, for instance) *and* introduce new skills. It will also press on expectations of form. Writing meant to be read on the Web, for example, may be shorter than other texts; it might be explicitly created in "chunks" that can be read in different orders based on how readers choose to follow the hyperlinks. Other Web-based products will leverage visual design to convey emphasis and help readers navigate the text. And in environments that aggregate many texts, effectively using titles, tagging, and creating summaries that appear in search windows will be essential skills. Few conventional rubrics will include or reward these skills or, even if they could, gauge the value of such skills in relation to other skills. What is, for instance, the technical as well as rhetorical value in being able to include a hyperlink as compared with the ability to craft an effective thesis statement?

Fortunately, as the field of digital writing comes to better understand and define the rhetoric of different digital environments, educators will be able to craft standards and assessment tools for classroom and institutional use that articulate effective practice in digital environments. It is likely, however, that large-scale assessments will take longer to develop because of the demands of designing, developing, and implementing effective and reliable assessments at scale. An example of such a large-scale assessment is the National Assessment of Educational Progress (NAEP) in Writing. In a very forward-looking move, the Framework Committees for the 2011 Framework in Writing and National Assessment Governing Board approved moving the NAEP in Writing to a computer environment beginning in 2011 despite the significant costs and logistical complications raised by making such a move. In 2011, students at the eighth- and twelfth-grade levels will compose on computers using commonly available tools, and students at the fourth-grade level will do so by 2019. The prompt for writing, however, and the rubrics utilized, will stress more conventional and accepted elements of writing that have typically been measured. Moreover, despite the opportunity to write with a computer, students will not be allowed to introduce visual or auditory elements into the text, thus negating the possibility of truly composing a digital text. In short, although students taking the NAEP will be writing on computers, they will not be engaged in the process of digital writing—which would incorporate audio, video, hypertext, and other digital elements. The process of developing, piloting, and refining tools for assessing emerging forms of multimodal composition in a large-scale environment is a task that still lies ahead.

E-Portfolios and Assessment

Some large-scale assessment programs are attempting to avoid the problems that often accompany large-scale assessment. For example, Kentucky's Commonwealth Accountability Testing System (CATS), highlighted in *Because Writing Matters* for its robust scoring guide, includes on-demand writing and a portfolio assessment. Distinct from a single on-demand writing test, a portfolio is a collection of writing done over time in a variety of settings. In Kentucky, the portfolio is ranked higher in importance than the on-demand writing. As Herrington, Hodgson, and Moran note in *Teaching the New Writing* (2009), few other states have adopted such a rich and writing-centered assessment process in the context of state accountability. Although the Kentucky procedures don't define expectations regarding digital portfolio creation, design, and management, Kentucky continues to provide a useful model for other states to consider, and a helpful template upon which others may build.

Digital technologies, with their capacity for expansive storage and ongoing revising and remixing of content, are an excellent match for portfolio-driven systems of assessment. A strong vision of how portfolios might evolve within the context of work on digital writing comes from Kathleen Blake Yancey, Kellogg W. Hunt Professor of English at Florida State University and former president of NCTE. In an edited collection titled *Electronic Portfolios 2.0: Research on Implementation and Impact* (Cambridge, Cambridge, and Yancey, 2009), Yancey and her colleagues Darren Cambridge and Barbara Cambridge discuss forays into what have been called "e-portfolios," beginning just a decade ago in the late 1990s and early 2000s. The authors focus on a wide-ranging set of institutions and individuals associated with the Inter/National Coalition for Electronic Portfolio Research, chronicling their developing approaches to e-portfolios and describing an emerging focus on lifelong-learning initiatives that make use of portfolios to offer a space to foster ongoing work and reflection.

Yancey describes the "tectonic" shift that we have experienced with digital technologies, and notes the compatibility between portfolio assessment and goals for digital writing (Yancey, 2009). Portfolios in teaching and assessment practices can move assessment from

1. The assignment and review of single, finished print texts to

2. The review of multiple print texts, including drafts of finished texts, inside a portfolio to

3. The review of multiple kinds of texts, digital and print, linking work inside school to that outside school and linking composers and texts to multiple contexts and audiences

E-portfolios allow for texts that are richly textured and layered, with elements of print pieces, spoken voice, visuals, and various digital composing processes visible across the work. They also allow students to document process, to show changes, and to explain decisions, and allow us to see a bigger range of their work than just a collection of finished pieces. E-portfolios, Yancey suggests, are a space for students to make visible so much of what is often invisible to readers, viewers, and even teachers themselves.

Like any portfolio, the e-portfolio is a collection of student work and accompanying reflection. In considering how to value what we see in an e-portfolio, Yancey offers a four-part framework (Yancey, 2009):

1. **Self-knowledge.** The knowledge writers have about their own writing practices; "of the kind of writer (e.g., single-draft, multi-draft, discovery) that he or she is, or used to be" and the ways in which the writer connects to the topic (both on paper and generally).

2. **Content knowledge.** The knowledge writers have about the topic that they have written about. This may be presented within a text, or in a reflective document that supplements the text. This reflection process answers the question "What did I learn?"

3. **Task knowledge.** The knowledge writers have about the processes and nature of writing, including "the role that audience and purpose play; strategies for developing a

persuasive argument; ways of voicing different kinds of texts; and ways of identifying rhetorical situations that call for different voices."

4. **Judgment.** The ability to reflect upon one's own work and address such questions as "Which paper [or multimedia piece] is your best? Which is your weakest? Why?"

Many of these elements become visible only across collections of student performances, and it is there that the e-portfolio comes into its own as an assessment approach. By providing teachers with a variety of digital compositions—created in different media and over time—e-portfolios allow students to demonstrate the depth and breadth of their abilities across the range of tools and contexts that we value in digital writing. Significantly, the e-portfolio itself can be a product that calls for the digital skills of remixing, managing, and organizing broad content, and shaping diverse elements for new purposes. In that sense, it is itself a digital composition.

New Technologies and Writing Assessment

As research on e-portfolios has demonstrated, longstanding principles of good writing assessment can guide us as we create more meaningful digital writing assessments. Technology can help solve problems of storage and search, and makes large collections of student work easier to manage. And Web tools make sharing and responding to student work easier.

In *Because Writing Matters,* we identified a set of components characteristic of high-quality assessment programs that support effective writing instruction. Here we look at how digital tools and technologies can enhance these components. We believe that the strongest assessment programs accomplish the following:

• Collect extended writing samples over time

Digital writing produced through blogs, wikis, and online word processing programs make it easier than ever for students to draft, revise, collect, and reflect on their writing over time. Students are able to copy, paste, and modify previous versions of their work and share it with peers and teachers for feedback. Teachers can then assess the revision process, as well as the final product, by looking at the history of revisions.

- Have students write in multiple genres

   Because of the many ways in which digital writing can be shared, aggregated, and circulated to real audiences, students can be encouraged to write about topics of personal interest in a variety of genres. In addition, students can write about topics in a variety of ways with different digital writing tools (for example, journaling on a topic with a blog, creating an article on a wiki, composing a slideshow presentation using an online creation tool). As multimedia authoring becomes a more prominent aspect of the digital writing process, students can create and embed images, audio, and videotexts in their work, and can both work within and extend existing types of writing. A personal memoir, for instance, can be transformed from a traditional essay into a digital story.

- Apply appropriate rubrics

   As digital writing continues to evolve, writing teachers can build on existing rubrics for models of how to assess student work, but must be conscious of the ways in which these rubrics may limit, or even contradict, the goals of digital writing. This situation, however, provides opportunities for teachers and students to more carefully name and explore the emerging conventions of digital writing. For example, what does it mean for a work of hypertext fiction to be "organized" or for a digital story to use "conventions" in contrast to what it might mean to look for organization and conventions in a traditional print essay?

- Address writing across content areas

   Supported by years of research that shows students need explicit instruction in how to write for the different discourses, genres, and conventions expected in diverse disciplines, digital writing tools give teachers in these content areas unprecedented opportunity to work with their students throughout the writing process. Moreover, when projects are constructed as collaborative writing assignments, content-area teachers and writing teachers could leverage the power of digital writing tools as networked writing spaces and work together to help students develop the content and form of their writing across classrooms.

In addition, Web 2.0 tools provide an expansive array of tools for teachers and students to communicate about their writing. For example, Richard Beach, Linda Clemens, and Kirsten Jamesen (2009) detail a wealth of approaches for providing formative feedback on students' digital work using synchronous and asynchronous tools, audio, and a variety of bookmarking and mark-up tools. For classroom assessment, the foundation for all assessment, Web 2.0 environments such as blogs or social networks provide analytic tools that can help students learn more about their audiences and these audiences' reactions. This process, in turn, helps students establish inquiry questions that they can follow with regard to their own work. Why does one post get picked up and circulated and another doesn't? Where do visitors come from? What links are most popular, and why might that be so? What do I learn from the comments visitors leave? Studying digital writing in this way invites students to use the same analytic tools that professionals use to better understand their own work and plan for its improvement. Analytic data do not provide an assessment, as there are many reasons for the results we see in community traffic and response to work on the Web, but in a supportive community of inquiry and response they can provide students and teachers with rich data to reflect on.

There are, of course, those who would suggest that technology *can* provide an assessment of student writing. Machine scoring of student essays is an expanding market in large-scale assessment, satisfying the desire for quick and efficient alternatives to labor-intensive processes of human scoring. In 2004, NCTE's Conference on College Composition and Communication (CCCC) issued their "Position Statement on Teaching, Learning, and Assessing in Digital Environments." In it, they make a strong case against machine scoring in favor of human readers, noting that

> because all writing is social, all writing should have human readers, regardless of the purpose of the writing. Assessment of writing that is scored by human readers can take time; machine-reading of placement writing gives quick, almost-instantaneous scoring and thus helps provide the kind of quick assessment that helps facilitate college orientation and registration procedures as well as exit assessments.

The speed of machine-scoring is offset by a number of disadvantages. Writing-to-a-machine violates the essentially social nature of writing: we write to others for social purposes. If a student's first writing experience at an institution is writing to a machine, for instance, this sends a message: writing at this institution is not valued as human communication—and this in turn reduces the validity of the assessment. Further, since we cannot know the criteria by which the computer scores the writing, we cannot know whether particular kinds of bias may have been built into the scoring. And finally, if high schools see themselves as preparing students for college writing, and if college writing becomes to any degree machine-scored, high schools will begin to prepare their students to write for machines.

For many teachers of writing, preserving the ethos of writing as a human act is essential, and machine scoring presents a counter-message that we may ignore at our peril. Others claim that the field of artificial intelligence that underlies machine scoring is developing at a rapid rate and in some interesting directions. As the collected authors of *Machine Scoring of Student Essays: Truth and Consequences* (Ericsson and Haswell, 2006) argue, if educators retreat from engagement in this field, companies like Vantage Learning, who market MY Access; or ETS, which offers Criterion; or Pearson, who markets Knowledge Analysis Technology, will insert themselves into large-scale assessment programs. And they will do so with relative ease, as the perceived efficiencies will probably be too great for overburdened administrators and institutions to ignore.

The challenge, of course, is in the larger field of standards, assessment, and accountability. Large-scale assessment programs have, in some cases, taken the "human reader" out of the assessment even where there is no machine scoring. As Liz Hamp-Lyons (2004) has written:

It is, unfortunately, true that much "direct assessment of writing" occurs in very sterile conditions: large exam halls, a one-size-fits-all prompt, 30 min to "write an essay," followed by mass scoring sessions at which any single student's text may be looked at by two individuals who each spend less than 60 seconds to reach a "judgment." AES [automated essay scoring] may do this job better than humans. But that's because the job itself is not intrinsically worth doing. As long as such pseudo-writing acts are required, perhaps we are better off giving them over to the machines. (265)

The reasonable concerns, and interest, that machine scoring introduces into the discussion of writing assessment may actually recede when we think about digital writing. New multimodal texts introduce semiotic systems and elements of communication that far outstrip the capacities of machine scoring to analyze. Images and audio cannot be handled the same way that words and sentences can. As we begin to value images, audio, and movement in digital writing, alternatives to human judgment may seem less enticing. More likely, the challenges of large-scale assessment of digital writing as a collaborative, interactive, multimodal practice will mean that accountability-focused assessment programs will be slow to incorporate the "new writing"—if they come to do so at all. For many teachers, such as Hodgson, Boardman, and the others whose stories and experiences we have included in this book, the promise of digital technologies is in the expansion of the human possibility to connect, communicate, collaborate, and create. Their hope is that more writing tasks and projects will be authentic work rather than the pseudo-writing acts required by current large-scale assessment programs. This understanding of the very human impulse to communicate and connect in a variety of forms is what needs to be preserved in the teaching, standards, and assessment of digital writing.

Professional Development for Digital Writing

Learning how to be a digital writer combines the both familiar and challenging process of writing with an added layer of complication that centers on rapidly changing and sometimes intimidating technologies. Taking the next step toward becoming a *teacher* of digital writing magnifies the challenge exponentially. Teachers need to plan for the diversities of students, their skills and interests in writing, and their familiarity with and access to digital tools both in school and at home. Teachers need to create healthy digital ecologies within the confines of technology support as it exists in their schools, and they need to wrestle with the complex problems and rich opportunities of curriculum design that situate digital writing within the larger set of learning goals for students. And all this needs to be undertaken in relationship to a field marked by rapid change. Given the complexities of teaching digital writing, imagine the complexities inherent in professional development programs that aim to support teachers working with digital writing in their classrooms.

In *Because Writing Matters,* we summarized lessons learned from decades of research on the characteristics of professional development that support teachers as they work to effectively implement complex instruction. This research continues to reinforce lessons about high-quality professional development articulated by the Consortium for Policy Research in Education over a decade ago (Elmore and Burney, 1997):

- Instructional change is a long, multistage process.
- Shared expertise is the driver of instructional change.
- Good ideas come from talented people working together.

These lessons, which also inform the National Staff Development Council's (NSDC) standards for professional development (2001), point to the need for *sustained* professional development that fosters ongoing, inquiry-oriented *learning communities* where educators are supported and challenged to examine student performance and pursue ambitious instructional change. However, as reported in the NSDC's 2009 report *Professional Learning in the Learning Profession: A Status Report on Teacher Development in the United States and Abroad,* "The kind of high-intensity, job-embedded collaborative learning that is most effective is not a common feature of professional development across most states, districts, and schools in the United States" (4). Drawing on significant research and cross-national data sets, the report presents the United States as lagging far behind other nations in providing public school teachers with opportunities to participate in such extended professional development.

If we are to substantially improve the teaching of digital writing, professional development must be central to our efforts. In relationship to technology, professional development does not serve to just enhance teachers' practices and maintain their pedagogical skill sets; professional development is also a key part of maintaining a healthy technological ecology. Because of the ways in which technologies emerge, evolve, and disappear, professional development to improve digital writing needs to go beyond a focus on technological skill development alone to include teacher leadership as part of the larger enterprise of technology development in schools or institutions of higher education. When technology changes or disappears, specific skills change. Investment in leadership lasts.

Many now agree that in the rush to and expense involved in upgrading our nation's schools and campuses to introduce information and communications technologies, professional development was sometimes an afterthought. Too often teachers received only enough training to be able to work the new equipment that showed up at the door. Fortunately, we have come to understand that a different kind of sustainable professional development is necessary. As the Consortium for School Networking (CoSN) affirms in *Digital Leadership Divide* (2009):

> [Professional development] is the next big milestone on the path to effective use of technology to improve teaching and learning. Clearly, as our survey findings show, school leaders overwhelmingly recognize that teachers need support in learning to integrate technology seamlessly into their classroom practices. Likewise, superintendents, principals and other administrators need an increased understanding of how technology can be wisely applied in school settings. Now is the time for school districts to make this a priority. (13)

Individual educators can and do pursue their own learning—and should be encouraged and supported to do so. However, planning for a coherent and thoughtful set of professional learning opportunities is a larger professional responsibility. Any model of professional development for digital writing should begin with principles that have been shown to be effective in linking professional development to overall community building, innovation, and instructional change. As argued in *Because Writing Matters*, professional development should be embedded in the job of teaching itself:

> Professional development can be school-based and homegrown. It can take place in the context of staff meetings and weekend retreats focused on studying specific strategies and topics, or in study groups built around surveying current writing and literacy research. These formats, however, should be an

integral part of a school's ongoing staff development plan and serve the larger goal of building an ongoing culture of instructional innovation in the school. (National Writing Project and Carl Nagin, 2006, 62)

This chapter explores the elements that support effective professional development of digital writing, linked to what we've discussed thus far in this book. We believe that the richest conceptions of professional development for improved teaching and learning will likely be informed by three key principles:

- People transcend tools; people should be primary.
- Good pedagogical practices transcend technologies; practice should be central.
- Designs for learning transcend designs for delivery; professional development should be learning focused.

With these principles in mind, we advocate three elements of high-quality professional development programs for digital writing, each of which is built on a strong foundation of personal experience, where teachers are invited to develop as digital writers and learners themselves. The section below on the first of these elements, Professional Development That Offers Opportunities to Develop and Reflect on Curriculum and Classroom Practice, connects to the early chapters in this book, in which we described the landscape for digital writing and explored what it means to learn to write digitally. The second element is described in the section titled Professional Development That Creates Opportunities to Work on Developing a Healthy Digital Ecology, which connects to Chapter Three's discussion of the need for healthy technological ecologies and some approaches to creating them. The third element is discussed in the section titled Professional Development That Examines the Standards and Assessment of Digital Writing, which links to Chapter Four. We conclude with a look at technology leaders who have created sustainable digital writing practices in their classrooms, schools, districts, and Writing Project sites.

Before we discuss these three elements, we will situate them with some foundational comments about effective practices for supporting teachers' work and ongoing professional development.

COMPLEX INSTRUCTION BUILT ON A FOUNDATION OF CONTENT-RELATED EXPERIENCE

When Kevin Hodgson, an elementary teacher introduced in Chapter Four and a member of the Western Massachusetts Writing Project, was searching for a tagline for his blog Kevin's Meandering Mind (see Web Resources), he settled on a quote from Charlie Parker: "If you don't live it, it won't come out of your horn." He explained, "This quote means a lot to me because it captures the concept that you have to live the world in order to understand it. As teachers, we don't often spend enough time exploring technology and writing ourselves before bringing it into the classroom. But I would argue that this kind of exploration is the key to understanding the possibilities for the learning and critical thinking of our students." An active writer and artist himself, Hodgson often uses his blog to create online experiences that will entice his colleagues into trying creative multimodal composing—all with a strong dose of playfulness.

Playful experimentation and engagement are as critical for teachers as they are for students, according to Elyse Eidman-Aadahl (2009) at the "Digital Is . . ." Convening:

> When we think back on the experiences that really led to powerful learning for us, they have the same characteristics we advocate for students, including an emphasis on real engagement. But sometimes we take such a serious and instrumental approach to professional development that we forget, or even suppress, the need we all have to play and experiment as we're learning something new. It seems counterintuitive, sometimes, for busy people like teachers to slow down, play, and experiment, but the insights we learn when we do are what help us teach for depth understanding.

For teachers of writing, this means the opportunity to work as a writer in a community of writers. Eidman-Aadahl continues, "We wouldn't want a science teacher to just lead students through a set of steps in an experiment with no deep engagement with science and the scientific method guiding their work as a teacher. Same with writing: it is often the experience of writing, creating, and inquiring, along with reflection on that experience, that helps move us beyond superficial instruction." Experience as a writer and participant in digital environments is foundational to the high-quality professional development that improves digital writing.

Teachers can, of course, gain experience with digital writing on their own through all the means available to any writer. They can set up blogs or podcasts, collaborate with others in wikis, participate in social networks, or create digital stories or mash-ups on their own using commercially available Web 2.0 tools. Multiuser blogging sites like Edublogs or social networks like Nings provide opportunities for teachers to use Web 2.0 tools in communities of like-minded and interested others. These environments go a long way toward promoting experience, but are not necessarily effective in facilitating reflection and learning in relation to that experience. One way to support professional development in digital writing is to create spaces in which teachers can quickly find the technical help and encouragement to use digital tools as writers within a context that also enhances collaborative learning, reflection, and inquiry.

Shelbie Witte, director of research for the Florida State University Writing Project, has been studying what happens when teachers are welcomed into spaces where they can learn about digital writing by doing it and reflecting on it. As a member of the NWP's E-Anthology team, Witte believes that responding, communicating, and connecting with fellow teachers in a digital environment can assist teachers as they learn to blend print and digital literacies and experiment with a range of technical tools. Witte's focus is the NWP's E-Anthology, an online national community where teachers can share their works in progress, discuss and create, ask for feedback, post revisions, and create portfolios of their work in connection with the face-to-face experience of local Writing Project summer institutes. Essential to the E-Anthology's success is that it is systematically integrated into an ongoing professional development experience. Witte notes that "being immersed in the technology and being surrounded by like-minded people who care about writing give participants the confidence to take a step beyond their comfort zone. There are people who are very comfortable doing that; they use technologies all the time. But I think that there is a big population of people who have never written online or used a wiki or a blog, and for the first time they are experiencing that." Knowing that there are systems of support and feedback is important during this acclimation and adoption process, as is tapping into a larger national audience that wouldn't otherwise be accessible.

Once teachers recognize that they are using the technology to support their work as writers, Witte observes, they become more comfortable with technology overall. "A lot of people think technology is going to take over and teachers aren't going to be needed anymore," Witte continues. "However, that's exactly where the teacher is needed, that's where the teacher comes into play. The digital environment can't replace conversations, tap creativity, and encourage writers. The technology does it to some extent, but not like a teacher does." Of course, conversations, creativity, encouragement, and support are also critical factors in successful professional development.

Another example of professional development that provides foundational experiences and reflection on digital writing comes from Michelle Rogge-Gannon, director of the Dakota Writing Project, who has developed what she calls a "digital writing marathon" for teachers. Rogge-Gannon calls the program a "marathon" to build off the more common experience of a "writing marathon," or an event where writers set aside time to write and respond intensively as a group, moving from place to place as they do so. The twist with a digital writing marathon is that the group writing is designed to move among different *online* environments rather than different *physical* environments. Rogge-Gannon describes one such marathon:

> The participants would perform writing tasks and explore a particular technology environment for one week. It could be, for example, digital storytelling, Nicenet, weblogs, Tapped In, wikis, or del.icio.us. We followed that on the next Monday night with an online synchronous discussion in Tapped In to discuss what their experience had been, what they had learned from it, and how it might be adapted for the classroom. (National Writing Project, 2008)

Rogge-Gannon's marathons continue throughout the year so that teacher-participants have time to think about the experience of their writing, get feedback and cocreate with colleagues, adapt what they are learning about writing into their classrooms, and share their findings with fellow marathoners. Key to the marathon, though, is the experience of writing in different environments, then reflecting on the experience. How is "wiki-ness" different from "blog-ness" or "synchronous chat"? What is it like to express yourself or collaborate with others using these different tools? When, as a writer, would you choose one environment over another? When, as a designer of collective projects, would you choose one over another? Through experiences like these, Rogge-Gannon believes, teachers can start to feel the affordances of different tools and environments from the inside and then bring that understanding into their teaching.

PROFESSIONAL DEVELOPMENT AS AN OPPORTUNITY TO INQUIRE INTO DIGITAL WRITING AND PRACTICE

These and other examples illustrate efforts to support teachers to develop the base of experience as digital writers that will be the foundation of their practice as *teachers* of digital writing. With the creation of this foundation as its objective, then, professional development can be designed to offer opportunities to pursue three essential elements of practice in teaching digital writing:

- Opportunities to develop and reflect on curriculum and classroom practice
- Opportunities to work on developing a healthy digital ecology
- Opportunities to consider standards and assessment of digital writing

We now examine in turn each of these three important elements, which together can create a high-quality professional development program for digital writing.

Professional Development That Offers Opportunities to Develop and Reflect on Curriculum and Classroom Practice

As we have demonstrated throughout this text, digital writing is complicated. Supporting teachers to become teachers of digital writing becomes even more complicated, as it leads to questions about students, curriculum, classroom, school, and community contexts—not to mention the technologies themselves. This process of examination is important and, ideally, intellectually stimulating.

Janet Swenson, past director of the Write for Your Life Project and founding director of the Red Cedar Writing Project, has seen the way that teachers can engage deeply with questions about digital tools and teaching. As she and her colleagues argue:

> [N]ew technologies are changing the types of texts we and our students create and interpret even as they are influencing the social, political, and cultural contexts in which our texts are composed and shared. Since these technologies are influencing the development of individuals, institutions, and communities (and since individuals, institutions, and communities are shaping these technologies and their uses), it is essential for English educators to turn a critical eye toward the benefits and affordances, the limitations and liabilities of integrating these newer technologies into our teaching. (Swenson, Rozema, Young, McGrail, and Whitin, 2005)

Examining technologies and their potential uses (as well as their pitfalls), then, should be a part of any professional conversation about digital writing. Swenson et al. point to the need for educators to take a critical stance toward implementing newer technologies and literacies rather than attempting to use technology for its own sake. Doing so requires professional development that cultivates, even welcomes, a critical stance toward the very tools it might be trying to promote.

Liz Stephens, former director of the Central Texas Writing Project and professor of Educational Technology at Texas State University San Marcos, agrees: "Trying to use technology doesn't mean throwing everything you've been doing out." Stephens has found that although practices do shift to accommodate particular tools like blogs and wikis, they nonetheless remain true to years of research and practice about supporting student writers: modeling and examining the processes writers use, examining purpose and audience for writing tasks, helping students find mentors and mentor texts in order to learn more about the art and craft of production, creating strong communities where collaboration and feedback can occur throughout the creative process, and providing productive formative and summative assessment of student work. For writing teachers who have already shifted their practice to center on student engagement and the coaching of student writers within a collaborative community, the shift to digital writing may feel like a strong positive extension of their current values—if they are supported to consider how the tools and the practices fit.

Bud Hunt, instructional technologist for the St. Vrain Valley School District and a teacher-consultant with the Colorado State University Writing Project, believes that it is often small shifts that can make the biggest difference in thinking through the practices of teaching digital writing. As a blogger himself, Hunt has explored the idea of "connective writing." He states, "The idea that texts online can begin to allow us to crystallize the connections between texts and between people in a way that offline texts cannot is, to me, one of the fundamental differences and important things about digital writing." Following through on significant ideas about digital writing and feeling free to take an inquiry stance about those ideas in relation to curriculum and practice are important prerequisites to making thoughtful decisions about technology.

Hunt describes one professional development initiative at a district level that he found particularly successful in supporting teachers to do just that: Cyber Camp. Offered over the summer as a paid professional development opportunity, this two-week session offers teachers a chance to learn about new technologies through terms that hearken back to early childhood pedagogy, but that work just as well for adults figuring out how to integrate technology into their teaching. From "play time" to "show and tell," Hunt maintains that this time is essential for teacher learning, because "you can't make a good decision [about what to use in your classroom] if you don't have good experience to influence your thoughts and actions, and that's larger than [just] technology."

Once he engages teachers in technology learning and digital writing practices, Hunt devises ways to support their work in the classroom. He insists that he is not a "tech support" person but an instructional technologist. His goals are larger and focused on helping teachers see that they are part of a network of shared inquiry about technology:

> My goal becomes to help teachers compose the thing, the idea of what they want to use. What is the actual learning objective that a teacher wants to accomplish? And then we sit down and go through the "OK, if this is what you want to do and this is why you want to do it, here are the three things you have to do." Then, I try to help folks see that it is not that you just turn on the technology and you're good to go, your kids are going to use it. More and more, I'll tell them, "Why don't you call this teacher at this school, because they have done this and you can see if that's what you want to do."

Along with helping teachers think broadly about their use of technology and connecting teachers to others interested in similar practices, as Stephens and Hunt do, professional development that attends to digital writing can also take up the lens of a particular curricular issue. This approach to professional development may look very different from an approach designed as a survey of new digital tools. Gail Desler, a technology integration specialist with the Elk Grove Unified School District and a teacher-consultant from the Area 3 Writing Project, describes a recent Enhancing Education Through Technology (EETT) grant that her district received to support work on multimodal writing in elementary classrooms. Desler began the project with a summer institute for teachers, highlighting some technologies they can use, such as blogs, wikis, and digital storytelling. But the real focus was preparation for a shared curricular project on the history of missions and missionary work in California, one of the state's social studies standards.

In this particular project, teachers developed inquiries focused on how using digital writing and technology allowed for critical approaches to the subject of missions in California. Taking her experience from an institute with the Holocaust Educators Network and blending it with a focus on how digital storytelling, in particular, can raise questions of perspective, Desler worked with teachers and students to move beyond the typical report on a particular mission to discuss elements of colonization and genocide. "There is technology, and then there is *technology*," Desler emphasizes. In this case, digital stories acted as a medium and a genre that allowed heightened attention to perspective as a critical concept in the study of the mission experience in California. For teachers, the experience is not of a project about technology, but of a project about important content that was deeper and richer because of technology.

In each of these cases, teachers are invited to extend their understanding of what it means to be a writer and teacher of writing given the digital tools they are afforded without losing sight of the core principles that guide their work: modeling good writing and responding to writers. As teachers then begin to understand the tools and are invited to make decisions about what they do, Hunt observes, "they start to become digital citizens, in a sense. They are willing to play in this new space. They are willing to write and learn in this space. You can see that they are active as learners. That passion is going to carry over into their work, even if they have technical hurdles." Passion and engagement are necessary ingredients for both personal learning and professional development. As we know, however, although a teacher's passion or the passion of a handful of teachers is enough to fuel a digital writing initiative, it is not enough—in isolation—to sustain a digital writing initiative. A larger, supportive ecology for digital writing is necessary to ensure continued work and ongoing professional development.

Professional Development That Creates Opportunities to Work on Developing a Healthy Digital Ecology

Richard (Dickie) Selfe has, for his entire career as a secondary educator and faculty member at Michigan Technological University and now at The Ohio State University, focused on developing sustainable technology-rich practices and spaces. A good deal of his work has been devoted to identifying best practices in technology professional development. In his book *Sustainable Computer Environments: Cultures of Support in English Studies and Language Arts* (2004; see also Selfe, 2003), Selfe admits that technology-rich instructional support is difficult to sustain because support programs

> require ongoing professional development programs and a
> commitment to innovation. They require constant monitoring

of students' literacy needs and skills. Teachers, administrators, and staff members must engage in continuous learning, experimentation, and formative assessment of their traditional duties. Often the leaders of technology-rich programs . . . need different kinds of support at different points in time and in their careers. If we acknowledge the fluid nature of technology-rich instructional environments and efforts, it should not surprise us that some explorations are short-lived. (x)

Selfe (2004) continues, however, by articulating the need to be experimental, to be innovative, and to engage in assessment. He encourages teachers, administrators, and staff members to be bold in the face of a shifting technological landscape while at the same time building mechanisms to protect the most-valued pedagogical goals and practices, and to preserve the overall infrastructure in which teachers, administrators, and staff members work. He observes that many of the schools with which he has worked operated within a "culture of blame," where stakeholders spend time casting blame for something not working (for example, a technology, a tool, an approach). In this context, people have very little time to devote to creating and sustaining a culture of support. Cultures of support, Selfe explains, prioritize people and their needs, and focus on creating, sharing, and assessing. Creating a culture of support requires four key investments:

- A supportive **planning process** through which instructors can build rich technology-intensive experiences for students and sustain those experiences;
- A **team of stakeholders** who recognize and value technological literacies;
- A **process of budgeting** for technology that is a living thing— that is, that has room to move and adjust as technologies change shape, break, or disappear; and
- A continual **program of assessment and redesign** to recreate and reinvigorate healthy technology-intensive programs. (xx)

Selfe's notion of a culture of support helps to illustrate how professional development can be embedded in larger processes of technology planning, instructional design, and collective planning. Technological competencies and expectations transcend specific disciplines, courses, and curricula, and therefore teachers, administrators, and other stakeholders share the responsibility of appropriately equipping students to engage in contemporary information and communication technologies. Teachers who have been given opportunities for strong professional development programs—programs that include access to tools, access to time, and access to other teachers—can pursue a next stage in their professional pathways by assuming some form of leadership in creating and sustaining healthy digital ecologies for their schools and institutions.

Patrick Delaney, associate director of the Bay Area Writing Project and librarian at Galileo Academy of Science and Technology in San Francisco, agrees with the importance of having faculty involved in solving the challenges of "time, infrastructure, and support" for digital writing. Delaney has worked with several teachers in the school to implement online national and international cross-classroom projects that connected students in history, social studies, and language learning (specifically Mandarin Chinese). His position as librarian, along with time and resource support from the school's last two principals, allowed him to work directly with teachers to design the needed infrastructure to support projects in individual classrooms. As Galileo Academy of Science and Technology is based in a historic building that needed considerable, and careful, attention, faculty and administration worked together closely to envision the digital ecology that would meet their needs. By 2009, Delaney points out, by working together the school had addressed the challenge of infrastructure. "We are now there," he reports, "we have the infrastructure we need. Four portable labs, a single-user login wireless network, fiber optic connection to the Internet, forty laptops in the library, etc." Delaney notes that the design of the infrastructure was informed throughout by faculty interested in the educational impact of technology decisions. He adds: "We always need to be asking the bigger question about technology—what do we want to do with it?"

Delaney knows that instilling a culture of writing in a school is "not a direct A-to-Z process"; rather, it is something that needs to be fostered and developed. Similarly, a culture that supports digital writing is cultivated by a strong, flexible infrastructure as well as time and support fostered by a robust leadership vision and ongoing community development. Galileo Academy now has some of this time and support in the form of teachers equipped to mentor colleagues, some of whom have schedules allowing for partner coaching; strong leadership to address programming and infrastructure development; and a shared commitment to working across content areas to understand better the affordances offered by access to what Delaney calls the "digital paper" that is now available.

And it's not just teachers and school administrators who can provide leadership. Students are also stakeholders in a culture of support. Selfe has championed the cultivation of student technology assistant programs as a key facet in both a healthy digital writing ecology and in teachers' professional development. Selfe (2004) describes four paths to integrating students in the culture of technology at a school:

1. **Independent-study programs**, where students are recruited to offer technology support or engage in technology-rich projects for academic credit

2. **Volunteer student-run workshops**, where students design and carry out workshops for other students and for teachers

3. **Programmatic integration**, where technology training for students is integrated in programs and curricula across classes, teachers, and approaches

4. **Work-for-pay programs**, where students work for the school as a professional technology support system

Student Technology Services (STS) at the University of Wisconsin–Milwaukee represents the fourth option above, and received an Educause Exemplary Practices Award in 2001. STS is staffed and managed entirely by students, who deliver technology support to the entire university. In this capacity students train, mentor, and supervise other students. Ongoing training and regular review are central components. The program's core principle is that "when students are entrusted with authority and decision-making capability, they will exercise it responsibly. The successful results have proven, again and again, that when given the opportunity, students will build confidence, self-improvement, and both personal and professional development." Owing to the success of the university's STS program, the model has been piloted in the Milwaukee Public Schools.

Another example, flexible enough to span the four program types above, is the Student Technology Leadership Program (STLP) in the state of Kentucky. Through the STLP, elementary, middle, and high school students are supported in developing skills to be technology leaders in their schools. Technology resources teachers support the students in learning a range of information and communication technologies, and then the students assist the resources teachers in developing and running workshops and providing one-on-one support to other students, teachers, and parents. Originally developed in 1994, the goals of the STLP are to

1. Develop activities that enhance the academic, social, and emotional growth of the student

2. Provide leadership opportunities for all students

3. Participate in multiage collaboration by forming innovative learning partnerships

4. Form learning partnerships among students with different technology skills

5. Develop activities that benefit communities

6. Develop instructional activities that integrate technology, benefit the school, and support the Kentucky Education Technology System (KETS)

In a recent report by the Appalachian Technology in Education Consortium (2007), reviewers noted the STLP's success, finding "overwhelming" enthusiasm on the part of students, along with enhanced technology-related skills and confidence. The report noted, "Students interact with teachers and other students at many different levels of technical proficiency, and are able to share their knowledge across usual boundaries of age, grade level, gender and culture."

Importantly though, student support programs can also be part of professional development for teachers. In the Kentucky example, teachers reported benefits that included increased use of and comfort with technology. The STLP also enhanced teachers' commitment to their schools and districts, with 25 percent reporting on a survey that their participation in the program "increased the likelihood that they will remain in the school system." The report writers call attention to this as an "amazing effect, considering the level of commitment STLP participation requires of them, and the fact that most of them receive no remuneration for this effort."

A more informal, but no less powerful, example comes from the Oregon Writing Project at University of Oregon, where teacher-leaders incorporate students into their professional development offerings. Project WRITE (Writing Revitalization through Integrated Technology and Enrichment), a professional development program focused on improving writing in high-need schools, provided workshops in digital storytelling for teachers in rural middle schools. These workshops were designed by teacher-leaders at the Writing Project and would start on a Friday evening, when teachers learned the basic software and discussed the potential of digital storytelling as an avenue for students' digital writing. Teachers would return Saturday morning and start to explore the movie-making tools by working on their own digital stories. As they did, they collaborated to develop a guide to digital storytelling to support and extend their own learning and their future teaching of digital storytelling practices and tools. Then, in the afternoon, the teachers would invite a couple of their students to join them and try out the guide. In no time, the students put together projects and suggested edits to the guidelines, preparing to work with their teachers to help lead their classmates in digital storytelling projects during the following week. According to Oregon Writing Project and Project WRITE director Lynne Anderson-Inman, "Students become involved in helping teachers with equipment and software, in planning for the class, and in taking other leadership roles. It becomes a partnership for teachers and a leadership opportunity for students."

These projects demonstrate that planning for and maintaining a healthy digital ecology can be considered everyone's business, not just the priority of beleaguered information technology departments or curriculum coordinators. By involving teachers and students in planning and leadership—and providing the professional development and operational support that allow them to play these roles—technology decisions can be directed more effectively toward purposes and experiences valuable for and valued by students. Although cloud computing and lower-cost hardware are helping make technology more affordable for schools, schools will still face significant costs and choices in creating digital ecologies, and their decisions will have instructional implications. If schools provision self-contained labs, faculty can be supported to effectively plan and organize instruction involving periodic visits to the labs. Students may experience highly developed lab instruction, but they won't necessarily experience the integration of technology into ongoing classroom-based instruction as they might in a 1-to-1 laptop environment or a program that makes use of mobile devices. These are distinctions that make a difference, and for that reason alone, support for learning about, reflecting on, and developing a digital ecology is an important element of professional development for teachers of digital writing.

Professional Development That Examines the Standards and Assessment of Digital Writing

In addition to a focus on teaching and learning and on digital ecologies, the third element in a well-developed plan for professional development is the opportunity to learn to assess digital writing and, consequently, to assess the quality and impact of various approaches to teaching digital writing. As Will Banks of the Tar River Writing Project suggests, "we [sometimes] get rewarded for just having the technology. And that is something that we have to be very careful about. To think that we are somehow doing something amazing just because we have a blog, or just because our students are making digital stories and using video, we can get suckered into the rhetoric of technology and progress." A high-quality professional development program should provide opportunities for faculty to study standards for and assessment of digital writing so as to make thoughtful decisions and provide effective responses to writers along the way and, ultimately, to reflect on these decisions informed by student work. This complicates but also enriches professional development efforts.

Ideally, engaging teachers in professional development that attends to the tools, approaches, and products of digital writing invites teachers into crafting better, more robust classroom practices through improved response and assessment. As we noted in the previous chapter, characteristics of digital writing, such as organizing through hyperlinks or creating chunks of content for Web delivery, represent emerging elements of writing. Other digital texts might include image and sound and, in doing so, shift conventional notions of how an essay is ordered and how it progresses. And the opportunity to study audience response through interactive digital environments provides direct windows into the rhetoric of digital writing. The fact that written products are changing in these ways means that teachers need a chance to revise their understanding of what it means to "write better." Similarly, the use of new tools that affect the practices of composing means that teachers need a chance to revise their understanding of the composing process. Our emerging knowledge of digital writing, then, needs to be connected to the key tools that teachers have for communicating ideas about quality: response and assessment.

Given that the field of digital writing is emergent, it provides an ideal setting for teachers and students together to engage in collaborative inquiry. Inquiry-oriented approaches to professional development, such as teacher research and action research, have a rich history in the profession and have been especially embraced by literacy teachers (Cochran-Smith and Lytle, 2009). Action research is a method that supports teachers and faculty in making and studying improvements in practice through cycles of action and reflective inquiry. This type of research is especially valuable for studying interventions in curriculum and teaching where teachers plan and study the development of their practice.

Inquiry-oriented approaches can also embrace more open-ended qualitative and naturalistic inquiry well suited to coming to understand new phenomena like digital writing and Web 2.0 environments. Involving students as co-researchers in digital writing can make for a powerful writing curriculum because it involves students directly in the phenomenon of interest. It can also produce important findings, as demonstrated, for example, by Michael Wesch's work with his students at Kansas State University. As discussed in the introduction, Wesch and his digital ethnography students have created and circulated influential analyses of digital culture as it is emerging in various online spaces, most notably represented through videos posted to YouTube (see Web Resources, Digital Ethnography Blog).

Teachers and students can also work together to understand, analyze, and improve their online experiences in educational settings. Both the teachers and the students connected to the Youth Voices online sharing space for digital writing (described in Chapter Three) benefit from working together to theorize about their shared learning space and to investigate what makes for more powerful student work. Their shared investigations make up a central practice that unites curriculum development, professional development, and teacher-student community.

Youth Voices describes itself as "a meeting place where students and their teachers share, distribute, and discuss their inquiries and digital work online. It's a space where teachers nurture student-to-student conversations, collaborations, and civic actions that result from publishing and commenting on each other's texts, images, audio, and video" (youthvoices.net). In order to keep this meeting space growing and authentic to its mission, both teachers and students are asked to reflect on their work within the forum and tag their reflections as "self-assessment" for others to share. Teachers share guidelines and suggestions for responding within the community, and students respond with comments and suggestions for further refinement, helping to develop a set of norms of participation within the forum itself. Teachers and sometimes students also discuss issues of developing community online, as well as thinking together about the design of the Youth Voices forum itself, via discussions on *Teachers Teaching Teachers* (see Web Resources), a weekly Webcast organized by many of the educators involved with the Youth Voices community (teachersteaching teachers.org). In one such Webcast, "What If You Ask the Students What They Think?" (October 2008), Youth Voices educators invited students with experience in a range of online environments to think with them about how best to support students in digital writing. Other shows, such as "Discussing Fundamentals and Building Plans Together" (March 2009), engage Youth Voices educators in reflecting on what is being learned and what questions are emerging from the work.

MOVING FROM "OVERCOMING RESISTANCE" TO "INVITING LIFELONG LEARNING"

In the first chapter we noted the danger of policy language that constructs teachers as technology-resistant digital immigrants reluctant to change. Such images of teachers do not inspire investments in professional development. Fortunately, there is ample evidence that given real opportunities to explore technology with a view to its potential to enhance learning for teachers and students alike, teachers can embrace and enjoy technology. When professional development addresses all the elements that support digital writing, change in classroom practice *can* happen.

This is one message Liz Webb, a teacher-consultant with the Red Cedar Writing Project (RCWP) at Michigan State University, would want everyone to hear. Webb and other teacher-leaders in Michigan were part of Project WRITE (Writing, Reading, Inquiry, and Technology Education), a professional development partnership between RCWP, four intermediate school districts, and two urban school districts. Project WRITE was developed as a sustained professional development opportunity that built a foundation in teacher experience of Web 2.0 tools, examined teaching and learning, investigated digital ecologies, and looked carefully at digital writing and student work. Webb notes that "in terms of what I saw from the beginning of the project to the end of the project, there was exponential growth in teachers' comfort level with using Web 2.0 applications, best practices [in writing instruction], and their willingness to make whatever effort was necessary to learn the new applications and find ways to take it to their classroom."

Originally conceived by three educators—Janet Swenson, director of the NWP's Technology Lead Site Team and associate dean of the College of Arts and Letters at Michigan State University; Sue Stephens, English language arts consultant with the Clinton and Shiawassee Intermediate Districts; and Troy Hicks, outreach coordinator of RCWP—Project WRITE sought to merge the research on adolescent literacy and newer technologies with effective professional development practices. Funded by a Title II Professional Development grant, forty teachers formed a learning community to closely examine student work with the intent of identifying materials and pedagogies that improve adolescent literacy and thoughtful integration of technology. Over the course of thirteen months, teachers met for ninety hours, including a one-week summer institute in August 2008. Teachers posted their writing, lesson plans, responses to professional texts, and teaching demonstrations on the Project WRITE wiki, thus creating an ongoing community of learning that utilized one of the digital writing tools they were using with their students.

Through professional development activities that modeled best practices in English language arts as well as such uses of the read/write Web as blogs, wikis, and podcasts, Project WRITE took an inquiry-based approach to teaching adolescent literacy with digital tools. According to Webb, teachers participating in the project felt nervous at first about using the technology, but over time they were able to improve their own skills and confidence, thus translating the work they did during the professional development sessions into their classrooms. Also, she noticed an important change for a number of teachers: "The thing that began to happen was that people began to help others in the project who maybe didn't understand a technological application quite as well," and this happened during organized sessions, as well as over e-mail, on the phone, and in one-to-one visits arranged outside of regular group meetings. "They were very gracious about [sharing their knowledge and expertise]," Webb states. Thus the project worked both to build capacity for teacher leadership and to develop processes for sharing questions and ideas. "The results are going to be very positive for students," Webb believes. "They have their teachers now teaching them in ways that utilize digital applications. I've been in the classrooms and I've seen them, and the result of this is that students are going to be better readers and writers."

While the examples in this chapter illustrate that there is no one right way to engage teachers in effective professional development, models such as those developed at the Red Cedar and Oregon Writing Projects demonstrate that learning about technology in the context of quality writing instruction, coupled with time for play and reflection, planning, and inquiry, can effect change in teachers' approaches to teaching with technology. But more than that, it can create learning communities that invite teachers to pursue more learning. When we plan professional development programs with the intent that they will be a first step in a longer journey of professional development, we are invited to reframe how we plan and organize learning experiences for ourselves and our colleagues.

Karen McComas and Felicia George, both of whom have served as chairs of the NWP's Technology Liaisons Network, are keenly aware of the importance of planning for long-term learning. McComas, associate professor of communication disorders and co-director of Marshall University Writing Project (MUWP), and George, associate director of the New York City Writing Project (NYCWP), have both been deeply involved in professional development related to digital writing for many years and have worked to coach others in designing professional development. Sometimes, as George observes, the challenges that local leaders face as they design professional development initiatives involving technology can appear to be nearly insurmountable. The diversity of skills and interests among teachers, the differences in technology provision at local schools, and the emergent nature of the field may seem too much to manage. As teachers are introduced to new technologies, it sometimes seems that "one little frustration in the area of technology" throws teachers off. And there will often be frustrations. Thus the professional development work that she and her colleagues in the NYCWP strive to provide aims straight for the heart of the matter: by introducing ideas that have value to teachers in the classroom, the NYCWP's professional development inspires and empowers teachers to use technology.

What this means at the NYCWP, then, is providing an interrelated set of long-term opportunities for technology learning that can be customized by teachers to meet a diversity of needs. In addition to connecting teachers to a wide range of networks and online learning opportunities, the NYCWP offers advanced summer institutes, school-year programs held on Saturdays, online experiences offered through their Web site, and the weekly Webcast *Teachers Teaching Teachers*. By engaging teachers across a variety of activities, both online and in face-to-face settings, the NYCWP offers teachers the opportunity to learn technological approaches and tools at a pace conducive to their own learning and to find colleagues to join them on the journey. Eventually, teachers begin to develop an inquiry stance toward technology in general. George says, "The more I play around with this stuff, the more I look at it as continually learning, as a new learning piece. And that's the kind of attitude that I like to see in teachers."

In a similar manner, McComas has seen growth happen, but not always as quickly or uniformly as some might expect from standard approaches to professional development with more traditional tools and methods. She notes a particular instance in which a teacher in one of MUWP's summer institutes resisted learning about blogging, yet a few years later wrote McComas a letter stating that she was using blogs in her classroom, with a great deal of success. "We provoke the conversations about teaching digital writing," McComas states, "then, we allow teachers time to play with the technology and incubate ideas." What happens over time, she suggests, is that teachers see how powerful technology can be in the lives of their students. "Many teachers just haven't thought about it. They sense there's something powerful [with technology]. They see things happening with their students that they don't see normally, such as when a student connects two images and makes a powerful statement by superimposing them. With technology, they see aspects of their students they are not [otherwise] able to see."

For McComas, then, opportunities can open up where we blur the lines between our personal and our professional lives. Sometimes, McComas says, we "compartmentalize technology. There is *school* technology and then there is *life* technology. And sometimes we really see those as different things." A powerful attitude shift begins to happen when teachers start to think about how digital writing tools such as blogs, photo sharing, and social networking—tools that students are likely to be using as a part of their everyday literacies—can be employed to enhance learning and collaboration in all facets of life.

An advantage of professional development related to Web 2.0 tools is that these same tools can be so useful in teachers' ongoing learning. As teachers develop skills and are encouraged to take an inquiry stance toward their practice, they often find that they are using their skills for their own continued learning. We can see this trend in the work of technology teacher-leaders, many of whom were early adopters and proficient users of Web 2.0 tools, as they sustain their learning through "personal learning networks."

A personal learning network (PLN), as discussed by educators such as Will Richardson on Weblogg-ed (2010), draws from this observation that the Web 2.0 tools that have ushered in new ways of reading and writing are the same tools that we as educators can use to connect to others who share our passions and that can help us become part of a network of colleagues interested in continuing professional growth. Lisa Nielsen, on her blog The Innovative Educator (2008), says,

> [P]ersonal learning networks are created by an individual learner, specific to the learner's needs, extending relevant learning connections to like-interested people around the globe. PLNs provide individuals with learning and access to leaders and experts around the world bringing together communities, resources and information impossible to access solely from within school walls.

In PLNs, teachers can pursue professional development that is individually tailored to their interests over long periods of time. Although PLNs are very familiar to educators in higher education, where forming and maintaining networks of colleagues are considered essential parts of being a professor, learning in this way is not often recognized or supported by K–12 schools and districts as professional development. But such networking should provide benefits to schools as well as individuals. As classic network theory (yes, people have been theorizing about networks since long before the digital social networking applications of today!) tells us, networks are stronger for having many links. More expansive and open networks, with many links and social connections, will bring more new ideas and opportunities to their members than closed networks where individuals circulate the same information. A group of individuals with broad connections and points of access to many social worlds will have access to a wider range of information. This core precept of network theory suggests that a school that supports faculty in cultivating and participating in a diversity of learning networks, and then in sharing their learning as colleagues involved in leadership in their building, would thus expand its professional learning exponentially.

Also significant to the teaching of digital writing is the fact that creating, managing, and leveraging a personal learning network is, essentially, an exercise in the skills, dispositions, and literacies that we seek to teach.

Navigating the Web, managing interactions on social networking sites, identifying mentors, and crafting an online identity are all at play in developing a PLN. This returns us to the foundational idea of professional development that provides teachers with authentic opportunities to be writers, learners, and participants. As Will Richardson has argued:

> [T]he power of the read/write Web is not the ability to publish; it's the ability to connect. Broken record, I know, but tools are easy; connections are hard. And so the question becomes how to best help educators realize these potentials in the learning sense first. Because at the end of the day, community building has to become an integral part of what we do in our classrooms with our students as well. We have to be able to model those connections for them and understand them in ways that are meaningful to our own learning practice. (2010)

Professional development that examines classroom practice, creates a healthy digital ecology, and deeply considers standards for and assessment of digital writing—especially within the context of healthy personal learning networks that teachers create so they, too, can learn how to use digital writing tools—can lead to changes that support digital writing.

Some Conclusions, Many Beginnings

In this book, we have explored what emerging digital tools and networked environments offer to writers now and into the future. We have relayed stories of teachers creating new teaching practices in ways that value the best traditions in the teaching of writing while exploring new possibilities. Finally, we have described elements of a healthy digital writing ecology, including implications for professional development, standards, and assessment. With all this in mind, however, we know that the human and technological networks within which we work will continue to change—and in ways that affect our teaching approaches, our social practices, and much more.

Early in this volume we pointed to one of Michael Wesch's Digital Ethnography videos. Another of his widely popular YouTube videos is titled *Web 2.0 . . . The Machine is Us/ing Us* (see Web Resources, Web 2.0). This video—which, as of February 2010, had been viewed on YouTube almost eleven million times—ends with the comment that today's digital spaces and networks are "linking people . . . people sharing, trading, and collaborating." As a result, it concludes, we will need to rethink a few things: copyright, authorship, identity, ethics, aesthetics, rhetorics, governance, privacy, commerce, love, family, ourselves. Not an easy task. And so with a view of the road ahead, in this afterword we focus less on conclusions and more on beginnings.

The practitioners, scholars, and opinion leaders cited in this book are not naïve. The potential effects of technology on education, as well as the potential for school reform that draws on technology, have been present for decades with arguably little effect. Researchers and critics alike note that despite the potential that technology holds, little substantive change has occurred in teachers' classroom practices. In short, for all the ways in which school technologies have been touted as "revolutionary," not much has changed for learners. We are, therefore, wary of entering a new contestant in the "oversold and underused" category (Cuban, 2001).

Yet for us—Dànielle, Elyse, and Troy—something feels significantly different at this *particular* moment, both in terms of the larger field and in terms of what we have learned in our talks with educators across the nation. The tools and environments we have been discussing in this book are not primarily tools for schools to manage their job, as currently constructed, more efficiently. They are not primarily tools for institutions at all. They are tools for learners and writers, and as learners and writers begin to use them across many areas of their lives outside of school, these tools will have a profound impact on the core business of life itself—and that is the core business that schools and writing classrooms attend to.

As we described in the preface, the idea for this book emerged in 2007 at a culminating conference for the NWP's Technology Initiative. At that conference, practitioners and scholars agreed that, as educators, we needed to move beyond popular concepts like "technology integration" (the notion that we need to put technology "into" teaching) if we were to invent new models and frames for the world we were just beginning to see. The world coming into view was one where technology was *already* "in" our teaching, our disciplines, and our lives. It was right in front of us; and we needed to better understand what that meant.

Two years later at another NWP conference—this one sponsored by the John D. and Catherine T. MacArthur Foundation's Digital Media and Learning Initiative—participants shared a deep and collective sense that we had made that move. At this conference, called the "Digital Is . . ." Convening, we saw that technology was everywhere, but the conversation was focused on writing, learning, and teaching where the presence of technology was taken for granted.

Collins and Halverson (2009) have suggested that American schooling, having emerged from an apprenticeship era into a universal schooling era, may be entering a third era: a lifelong-learning era in which institutional, social, and technological innovations are leading people to "extend learning throughout life and over many venues" (89). If true, this era will be enabled by new technologies, but it won't be *about* those technologies. What may make the work of this generation of technology in schools different from that of previous ones is the interest in looking at what the tools do for engaged learners/writers/creators rather than for institutions. This world— one in which digital tools and spaces offer opportunities for integrated, rich, and critical learning, writing, creating, and more—is just now becoming visible. So, instead of concluding with a series of recommendations for administrators and other stakeholders as *Because Writing Matters* did, we focus here on the strong beginnings that we saw emerging at the "Digital Is . . ." Convening—beginning with what the future of digital writing might look like in a world where, quite simply, digital is the way we write and learn.

BEGINNINGS: SCHOOLS EMBRACING CHANGE AND EDUCATING FOR THE FUTURE

Right now, it may be more common for individual teachers to focus on digital writing than for whole schools to do so. But this may be changing. And indeed, if we are to develop healthy digital ecologies for learning that support teachers and students, our focus must broaden. Models for schools that embrace technology as a tool for learning are beginning to emerge, and as we look more closely at them we can start to see the beginnings of what it would look like for schools to create a strong digital ecology yet still keep a focus on our core values related to learning. At the "Digital Is . . ." Convening, educators Zac Chase, Diana Laufenberg, Melanie Manuel, and Gamal Sherif, and students from the Science Leadership Academy (SLA) in Philadelphia, provided a picture of what one such school might look like.

The SLA speakers noted that there is a point where educators can get lost in choosing a particular technology tool, raising questions that range from

"Should I use a blog or a wiki?" to "How much will my students already know about this tool and its use?" After several years of developing their program, however, SLA principal Chris Lehmann and his staff are clear that these are not the questions that guide teaching and learning.

For Lehmann and his colleagues, digital writing needs to be organic to the task at hand. Usually, the tools put to use are chosen at the point of need, not before. He elaborates:

> When you have strong, well-structured, scaffolded projects, and the pedagogy is based on deep understanding, then it's not that scary that a kid might say, "I want to use Keynote," and another kid might say, "I want to use Slideshare." Who cares? The question is "What are you doing?" The tools today are pretty easy and not that hard to learn. I think that the more scary ones are when you say, "OK, for this project, we are all going to do this one thing."

Featured by *Edutopia* as a model for integrating technology, SLA "provides a rigorous, college-preparatory curriculum with a focus on science, technology, mathematics and entrepreneurship" (Smith, 2007). Within this curriculum, as Lehmann notes, learning how to use digital writing tools is not the primary focus of classroom instruction or professional development. Instead, pedagogy and curriculum take center stage, and this ethos permeates the school's daily work and its Web site, www.scienceleadership.org.

Embodied in this approach are the core principles of SLA's pedagogical stance. Teachers integrate elements of inquiry, research, collaboration, presentation, and reflection into all unit plans, building from *Understanding by Design* (Wiggins and McTighe, 2005). Rather than starting with discussions about technology, SLA teachers collaborate by talking about teaching first. Lehmann explains that teachers ask one another key questions: "What are you doing?" "What are your goals?" and "What's the tool that works?" He believes that a wiki works well for group projects, blogs archive an individual's thoughts, and forums can allow for threaded discussions over time—all of which support different pedagogical goals.

"Kids are writing all the time, and in some way, shape, or form, they are writing publicly," notes Lehmann. He differentiates the type of writing that students at SLA engage in from what he sees in other school contexts:

> So much of the writing is about more than teacher-student interaction. In so many schools, the writing process is closed. It is a dialogue between teacher and student and nothing else. It is our experience that the more ways that writing becomes a collaborative process, the more ways that you are writing for a different audience, the more powerful that can be.

Collaboration occurs between SLA students, teachers, and outside experts and community members. In this writerly configuration, digital writing tools enable students to build learning networks inside and outside the classroom.

It goes without saying that change happens slowly; for Lehmann, focusing on change through the use of digital writing tools alone misses the point, as it will not transform pedagogy. Instead, he suggests that teachers and students use digital writing tools to meet their own teaching and learning needs. Lehman recommends room for learning and play, supportive systems that focus on people above tools, and rewards for success and understandings of failure:

> When there is a sense of collaboration, when there are times that you set aside in faculty meetings to share unit plans and ideas, and critique each other's work, you create an environment where sharing around the digital stuff can happen. I think that the trick is that it's not like you say, "All right, everybody share best practices on the tech." We talk about sharing best practice about teaching and learning.

As the students at SLA continue to deepen their understanding of literature, math, history, science, the arts, and how to choose a college and career, the faculty continue to learn and grow their capabilities with newer technologies, implementing digital writing throughout the curriculum and creating substantive opportunities for teaching and learning. "You've got to be very thoughtful, and cautious, and smart about the way you move forward," concludes Lehmann. "You do have to realize this is not additive; this is transformative pedagogy."

SLA is in a position similar to that of other schools in the High Tech High network in Southern California or the New Tech Network of schools, a forty-school network across the United States. Once faculty have come to understand the affordances of these new tools and have shaped effective digital ecologies, the central issues for schools to address continue to be the development of rich curricula; the opportunities for students to do important and engaging work; and the thoughtful guidance, response, and leadership that wonderful faculty can provide.

BEGINNINGS: LINKING IN-SCHOOL TIME AND OUT-OF-SCHOOL TIME TO SUPPORT MORE POWERFUL LEARNING OPPORTUNITIES

One of the more powerful affordances of new digital environments is that they are typically "on" 24/7/365. For learners and writers who have appropriate access to online learning environments at home and in the community, the opportunity to extend learning time is very real. Not all students, however, have such access. Some may have access to tools, but not to mentors or experts in areas they hope to learn about. Others may lack access to models, examples, and inspiration. Schools can seek to remedy this by providing access and mentors, but they can't easily add minutes to a school day already strained under the pressures of standards and accountability measures. The pressures of time are particularly acute for young people seeking to learn labor-intensive skills like video and audio editing, which demand both access to equipment and lots of time.

Nichole Pinkard, visiting associate professor at the College of Computing and Digital Media at DePaul University, founded the Digital Youth Network (DYN) in Chicago based on the idea that schools alone cannot be expected to provide full support for students as media creators. Instead, by blending in-school and out-of-school learning opportunities, educators can create much more powerful contexts for students to learn digital writing and media creation. Working intensively with teachers and community mentors, the Digital Youth Network has created a curriculum that spans the school day and then links to an after-school program that extends the learning day. According to DYN teachers Tene Gray and Tracy Lee, the curriculum "enables teens to become discerning new media consumers and fluent new media producers."

At DYN, students' composing and production practices are shaped around four main objectives:

- The first objective is to ensure that teens posses a fundamental understanding of the various modes of communication that comprise the new media landscape.

- The second objective is rooted in the realization that students learn the methods associated with each mode of communication most powerfully when they take on multiple tasks in the creation of new media artifacts.

- The third objective is to ensure that teens are able to think critically about the meaning of new media messages as both consumers and producers.

- The fourth objective is to imbue teens with a core set of values needed to become productive and prosperous citizens in the twenty-first century.

At DYN, a careful pairing of in-school and after-school programs allows students to work intensively on media products and provides access to artists and mentors from the community who can coach advanced production skills for students. In addition, DYN hosts a dedicated online social network called Remix World (iremix.org) designed for young people to share their media products, seek response and feedback, and eventually publish.

In response to the DYN presentation at the "Digital Is . . ." Convening, Laura Roop, an outreach project manager at the University of Michigan and director of the Oakland Writing Project, noted the power that the extra time and connection to community mentors provided for the young people participating in DYN's programs. She observed that across the divide that typically separates in-school and out-of-school practitioners, the adults working with youth "really understand new media literacies, and are assisting youth to become powerful creators who can consciously take multiple roles, from builder to performer to writer to innovator to critic, with relation to these media." Students, she said, consumed and created media, with digital writing tools integral to that process, and along the way they were able to develop critical capacities that went well beyond superficial acquaintance with digital composing. They were also able to understand the circulation of media products and to imagine what it might be like to manage new media as a career or business.

BEGINNINGS: NETWORKING PARTNERS TO NETWORK LEARNING OPPORTUNITIES

As the work of the teachers and community partners at the "Digital Is . . ." Convening illustrated, school is just one node in a (potentially global) learning network that young people have the opportunity to inhabit. Linking in-school and after-school activities helps expand the learning network. In many communities, there is an extensive range of institutions that work with young people, such as museums, libraries, community-based organizations and nonprofits, and higher education institutions. New digital tools offer opportunities to link the assets and programs of community institutions in new ways, ways that both extend their individual missions and also provide a more integrated experience for young people.

In New York City, for example, youth-serving organizations are working together to create the New Youth City Learning Network (newyouthcity.net). By leveraging their collective experience, resources, programs, and digital assets, the museums, libraries, and youth-serving organizations in the New Youth City Learning Network hope to create ever more powerful learning opportunities for young people. Similarly, institutions in Chicago, Pittsburgh, and other cities have been working together to explore how to create networks across institutions that put young people at the center.

Whereas networks such as those in New York pull together institutions in a physical space, it is also possible to network institutions across distant places into integrated learning experiences. The programs offered by another organization, Global Kids, illustrate how partnering to create learning experiences while taking advantage of the affordances of digital environments can create new kinds of experiences for young people. Speaking at the "Digital Is . . ." Convening, Global Kids took the audience into the project I Dig Zambia, created out of a partnership between Global Kids in New York City and the Field Museum in Chicago (see Web Resources, I Dig Science). In I Dig Zambia, museum educators, field scientists, teachers, and students collaborate with read/write Web tools such as blogs, wikis, and Skype as well as through virtual worlds such as Second Life to engage students in paleontology, connecting them to real-time fossil digs in Africa. Students visited museum environments from home, conferred with scientists in the field about their daily accomplishments, and modeled a "dig" in a virtual environment. Like the teachers and students at SLA, participants in the I Dig Zambia experience do not begin with the question of which digital writing tools to use; instead, they focus on the process of scientific inquiry and choose tools that will help them experience, as completely as possible, the work of paleontology, collaborating with each other and with experts to develop multimedia compositions that represent what they have learned.

As we imagine the possibilities for digital writing, we look at programs like I Dig Zambia to inspire our thinking about what can happen in our schools and classrooms, thinking carefully about the affordances and constraints, the challenges and opportunities that digital writing ecologies can bring to our teaching and to student learning. These examples point to emerging directions and promising practices, the sense of an exciting new future.

But they also represent an extension of the approaches and practices that teachers of writing and the National Writing Project have long advocated: honoring the power of writing in the world, giving young people the opportunity to do real work as writers with the faith that they can rise to the occasion, engaging the adults who work with youth to cross the boundaries of institutions, grade levels, and subject areas to improve practice.

Because Writing Matters concludes by calling for a "paradigm shift away from the limited view of writing as a discrete subject area of the exclusive domain of English language arts instruction" (National Writing Project and

Carl Nagin, 2006, 105) and argues that writing matters, both in school and out, as an academic achievement and, more important, as a lifelong capacity. As students learn how to think and ask questions; how to read and think critically about information they encounter; and, most important, how to play active roles in our democratic society, we build more than our schools: we build our future.

Here we conclude by echoing the call from that earlier book and by reiterating that, more and more, our students are learning to think, to read, and to ask questions in networked environments, enabled by computers, mobile phones, e-book readers, and other technologies. They will encounter information requiring them to think critically, because information travels quickly, in multiple modes, in many different directions. They have the potential to make a first movie as easily as they will write a first story. With a global audience, they can publish insight and wisdom, and they can publish misinformation and inanities. In short, we need to do what we have always done as educators: guide and respond to our students' writing even though technologies continue to change. We encourage students, teachers, administrators, community partners, and all others with a stake in creating a society in which we can all play active roles in our democratic future, to join in writing our future *together*. What we do as teachers matters because—in the world our students will create and inhabit—digital writing matters.

NOTES

Introduction

Belden Russonello & Stewart. (2007). *The 2007 Survey on Teaching Writing—American Public Opinion on the Importance of Writing in Schools*. Conducted for the National Writing Project. Washington, DC: Belden Russonello & Stewart.

DeVoss, Dànielle Nicole, and Dickie Selfe. (2002). "Encouraging and Supporting Electronic Communication Across the Curriculum Through a University and K–12 Partnership." *Computers and Composition 19*(4), 435–51.

Eidman-Aadahl, Elyse. (2009, November 18). "Reimagining Literacy in the Digital Age." Opening remarks at the "Digital Is . . ." Convening, Philadelphia, PA.

Fisch, Karl, and Scott McLeod. (2007). *Did You Know?: Shift Happens*. Retrieved December 21, 2008, from www.youtube.com/watch?v=pMcfrLYDm2U&feature=related.

Haas, Angela. (2008). *What American Indians Can Tell Us About Memoria, Hypertext, Visual and Digital Rhetoric, and Technical Communication*. Unpublished doctoral dissertation. Michigan State University, East Lansing, MI.

Ito, Mizuko, Heather Horst, Matteo Bittani, danah boyd, Becky Herr-Stephenson, Patricia G. Lange, C. J. Pascoe, and Laura Robinson. (2008). *Living and Learning with New Media: Summary of Findings from the Digital Youth Project*. John D. and Catherine T. MacArthur Foundation Reports on Digital Media and Learning. Available at digitalyouth.ischool.berkeley.edu/files/report/digitalyouth-WhitePaper.pdf.

Jenkins, Henry, Kate Clinton, Ravi Purushotma, Alice J. Robinson, and Margaret Weigel. (2006). *Confronting the Challenges of Participatory Culture: Media Education for the 21st Century*. John D. and Catherine T. MacArthur Foundation occasional paper on digital media and learning. Available at digitallearning.macfound.org/atf/cf/{7E45C7E0-A3E0-4B89-AC9C-E807E1B0AE4E}/JENKINS_WHITE_PAPER.PDF.

Joseph, Chris. (2005). State of the Art. trAce Online Writing Centre. Retrieved August 30, 2008, from tracearchive.ntu.ac.uk/Process/index.cfm?article=131.

Lenhart, Amanda, Sousan Arafeh, Aaron Smith, and Alexandra Rankin Macgill. *Writing, Technology and Teens*. (2008, April). Pew Internet & American Life Project, with the National Commission on Writing. Retrieved from www.pewinternet .org/~/media//Files/Reports/2008/PIP_Writing_Report_FINAL3.pdf.pdf.

National Commission on Writing for America's Families, Schools, and Colleges. (2003). *The Neglected "R": The Need for a Writing Revolution*. Retrieved December 21, 2008, from www.writingcommission.org/prod_downloads/writingcom/neglectedr.pdf.

National Commission on Writing for America's Families, Schools, and Colleges. (2004). *Writing: A Ticket to Work . . . Or a Ticket Out: A Survey of Business Leaders*. Retrieved July 17, 2010, from www.collegeboard.com/prod_downloads/writingcom/writing-ticket-to-work.pdf.

National Council of Teachers of English. (2007). *21st Century Literacies: A Policy Research Brief Produced by the National Council of Teachers of English*. Retrieved December 21, 2008, from www.ncte.org/library/NCTEFiles/Resources/PolicyResearch/21stCenturyResearchBrief.pdf.

National Council of Teachers of English. (2008a, November). *NCTE Framework for 21st Century Curriculum and Assessment*. Retrieved December 21, 2008, from www.ncte.org/governance/21stcenturyframework?source=gs.

National Council of Teachers of English. (2008b). *Writing Now: A Policy Research Brief Produced by the National Council of Teachers of English*. Retrieved December 21, 2008, from www.ncte.org/library/NCTEFiles/Resources/PolicyResearch/WrtgResearchBrief.pdf.

National Writing Project and Carl Nagin. (2006). *Because Writing Matters: Improving Student Writing in Our Schools* (Rev. ed.). San Francisco: Jossey-Bass.

Selber, Stuart. (2004a). *Multiliteracies for a Digital Age*. Carbondale: Southern Illinois University Press.

Selber, Stuart. (2004b). "Technological Dramas: A Metadiscourse Heuristic for Critical Literacy." *Computers and Composition 21*, 171–95.

Wesch, Michael. (2007). *A Vision of Students Today*. Retrieved December 21, 2008, from www.youtube.com/watch?v=dGCJ46vyR9o.

Writing in Digital Environments (WIDE) Research Collective. (2005). "Why Teach 'Digital Writing'?" *Kairos: A Journal of Rhetoric, Technology, and Pedagogy 10*(1). Retrieved December 21, 2008, from english.ttu.edu/Kairos/10.1/coverWeb/wide/index.html.

Chapter One

Besser, Howard. (2001). "The Next Digital Divides." *Teaching to Change LA (TCLA) 1*(2). Retrieved October 17, 2008, from tcla.gseis.ucla.edu/divide/politics/besser.html.

Center for Digital Storytelling. (n.d.). Retrieved December 18, 2008, from www.facebook.com/group.php?gid=2394979784.

Center for Media Literacy. (n.d.). *Literacy for the 21st Century: An Overview & Orientation Guide to Media Literacy Education.* Retrieved May 19, 2009, from www.medialit.org/reading_room/article540.html.

Center for Social Media, School of Communication, American University. (n.d.). *Code of Best Practices in Fair Use for Media Literacy Education.* www .centerforsocialmedia.org/fair-use/best-practices/media-literacy.

Cuban, Larry. (1986). *Teachers and Machines: The Classroom Use of Technology Since 1920.* New York: Teachers College Press.

Cuban, Larry. (2001). *Oversold and Underused: Computers in the Classroom.* Cambridge, MA: Harvard University Press.

DeVoss, Dànielle Nicole, and Dickie Selfe. (2002). "Encouraging and Supporting Electronic Communication Across the Curriculum Through a University and K–12 Partnership." *Computers and Composition 19*(4), 435–51.

Hargadon, Steve. (2007). "A 14-Year-Old Talks Educational Technology." *K–12 Educational Technology,* October 19, 2007. www.stevehargadon.com/2007/10/ 14-year-old-talks-educational.html.

International Society for Technology in Education. (n.d.). *National Educational Technology Standards (NETS) for Students 2007.* Retrieved May 19, 2009, from www.iste.org/AM/ Template.cfm?Section=NETS.

Ito, Mizuko, Heather Horst, Matteo Bittani, danah boyd, Becky Herr-Stephenson, Patricia G. Lange, C. J. Pascoe, and Laura Robinson. (2008). *Living and Learning with New Media: Summary of Findings from the Digital Youth Project.* John D. and Catherine T. MacArthur Foundation occasional paper on digital media and learning. Available at digitalyouth.ischool.berkeley.edu/files/report/digitalyouth-WhitePaper.pdf.

Jenkins, Henry, Kate Clinton, Ravi Purushotma, Alice J. Robinson, and Margaret Weigel. (2006). *Confronting the Challenges of Participatory Culture: Media Education for the 21st Century.* John D. and Catherine T. MacArthur Foundation occasional paper on digital media and learning. Available at digitallearning .macfound.org/site/c.enJLKQNlFiG/ b.2108773/apps/nl/content2.asp?content_ id={CD911571–0240–4714-A93B-1D0C07C7B6C1}&notoc=1.

Lankshear, Colin, and Michele Knobel. (2006). *New Literacies: Everyday Practices and Classroom Learning* (2nd ed.). Maidenhead, NY: Open University Press.

Lenhart, Amanda, Sousan Arafeh, Aaron Smith, and Alexandra Rankin Macgill. *Writing, Technology and Teens.* (2008, April). Pew Internet & American Life Project, with the National Commission on Writing. Retrieved from www.pewinternet.org/~/media//Files/Reports/2008/PIP_Writing_Report_FINAL3.pdf.pdf.

Lessig, Lawrence. (2005). *Free Culture: The Nature and Future of Creativity.* New York: Penguin.

Lessig, Lawrence. (2008). *Remix: Making Art and Commerce Thrive in the Hybrid Economy.* New York: Penguin.

Mishra, Punya, and Matthew J. Koehler. (n.d.). TPACK Wiki. www.tpack.org/tpck/index.php?title=Main_Page.

Mishra, Punya, and Matthew J. Koehler. (2006). "Technological Pedagogical Content Knowledge: A New Framework for Teacher Knowledge." *Teachers College Record 108*(6), 1017–54.

National Council of Teachers of English. (2008, November). *NCTE Framework for 21st Century Curriculum and Assessment.* Retrieved December 21, 2008, from www.ncte.org/governance/21stcenturyframework?source=gs.

Oppenheimer, Todd. (2003). *The Flickering Mind: The False Promise of Technology in the Classroom, and How Learning Can Be Saved.* New York: Random House.

Partnership for 21st Century Skills designed in cooperation with the National Council of Teachers of English. (n.d.). *21st Century Skills Map: English.* Retrieved May 19, 2009, from www.21stcenturyskills.org/documents/21st_century_skills_english_map.pdf.

Porter, Bernajean. (2005). *DigiTales: The Art of Telling Digital Stories.* Denver, CO: bjpconsulting. www.digitales.us/.

Prabhu, M. (2008, October 21). "'Digital Disconnect' Divides Kids, Educators." *eSchool News.* Retrieved December 21, 2008, from www.eschoolnews.com/news/top-news/ index.cfm?i=55665.

Prensky, Marc. (2001, October). *Digital Natives, Digital Immigrants*—Part 1. Retrieved December 21, 2008, from www.marcprensky.com/writing/Prensky%20-%20Digital%20Natives,%20Digital%20Immigrants%20-%20Part1.pdf.

Vaidhyanathan, Siva. (2008, September 19). "Generational Myth: Not All Young People Are Tech-Savvy." *Chronicle of Higher Education: Chronicle Review.* Retrieved October 12, 2008, from chronicle.com/free/v55/i04/04b00701 .htm?utm_source=cr&utm_medium=en.

Writing in Digital Environments (WIDE) Research Collective. (2005). "Why Teach 'Digital Writing'?" *Kairos: A Journal of Rhetoric, Technology, and Pedagogy 10*(1). Retrieved December 21, 2008, from english.ttu.edu/Kairos/10.1/coverWeb/wide/index.html.

Chapter Two

Beach, Richard, Chris Anson, Lee-Ann Kastman Breuch, and Thom Swiss. (2008). *Teaching Writing Using Blogs, Wikis, and Other Digital Tools.* Norwood, MA: Christopher-Gordon.

Besser, Howard. (2001). "The Next Digital Divides." *Teaching to Change LA (TCLA) 1*(2). Retrieved October 17, 2008, from. tcla.gseis.ucla.edu/divide/politics/besser.html.

Center for Social Media, School of Communication, American University. (n.d.). *Code of Best Practices in Fair Use for Media Literacy Education*. www .centerforsocialmedia.org/fair-use/best-practices/media-literacy.

Copyright-Friendly and *Copyleft* Images and Sound (Mostly!) for Use in Media Projects and Web Pages, Blogs, Wikis, etc. (n.d.). copyrightfriendly.wikispaces.com/.

Elbow, Peter. (1998a). *Writing Without Teachers* (2nd ed.). New York: Oxford University Press.

Elbow, Peter. (1998h). *Writing with Power* (2nd ed.). New York: Oxford University Press.

Graham, Steve, Charles A. MacArthur, and Jill Fitzgerald. (2007). *Best Practices in Writing Instruction*. New York: Guilford Press.

Graham, Steve, and Dolores Perin. (2007). *Writing Next: Effective Strategies to Improve Writing of Adolescents in Middle and High Schools—A Report to Carnegie Corporation of New York*. Washington, DC: Alliance for Excellent Education. Retrieved September 13, 2009, from www.all4ed.org/files/WritingNext.pdf.

Herrington, Anne, Kevin Hodgson, and Charles Moran (Eds.). (2009). *Teaching the New Writing: Technology, Change, and Assessment in the 21st-Century Classroom*. New York: Teachers College Press; Berkeley, CA: National Writing Project (copublished).

Hicks, Troy. (2009). *The Digital Writing Workshop*. Portsmouth, NH: Heinemann.

Ohler, Jason. (2009). "Orchestrating the Digital Collage." *Educational Leadership* 66(4), 8–13.

Palmquist, Mike. (2003). "A Brief History of Computer Support for Writing Centers and Writing-Across-the-Curriculum Programs." *Computers and Composition* 20(4), 395–413.

Valenza, Joynce. (n.d). "Joyce Kasman Valenza." www.sdst.org/shs/library/jvweb .html.

Chapter Three

Brown, Malcolm. (2005, July/August). "Learning Space Design Theory and Practice." *EDUCAUSE Review* 40(4), 30.

Center for Social Media, School of Communication, American University. (n.d.). *Code of Best Practices in Fair Use for Media Literacy Education.* www.centerfor-socialmedia.org/fair-use/best-practices/media-literacy.

Childers, Pamela. (2004). "Interacting with Computer Technology in Secondary Schools." *Computers and Composition* 20(4), 473–80.

Chism, Nancy Van Note. (2006). "Challenging Traditional Assumptions and Rethinking Learning Spaces." In Diana G. Oblinger, *Learning Spaces*, 2.1–2.12. Educause. Retrieved January 28, 2009, from www.educause.edu/Learning Spacesch2.

Common Sense Media. (n.d.). Digital Literacy and Citizenship Curriculum. www.commonsensemedia.org/how-be-common-sense-school2.

Global Kids, the Goodplay Project at Harvard University's Project Zero, and Common Sense Media. 2009. *A Meeting of the Minds: Cross-Generational Dialogues on the Ethics of Digital Life.* www.globalkids.org/meetingofminds.pdf.

Hunt, Bud. (2005). Sample Blog Acceptable Use Policy. www.budtheteacher.com/wiki/index.php?title=Sample_Blog_Acceptable_Use_Policy.

James, Carrie. (2009). *Young People, Ethics, and the New Digital Media.* John D. and Catherine T. MacArthur Foundation. Available at mitpress.mit.edu/catalog/item/default.asp?ttype=2&tid=12009&mode=toc.

Johnson, Chris, and Cyprien Lomas. (2005, July/August). "Design of the Learning Space: Learning and Design Principles." *EDUCAUSE Review 40*(4), 16–28.

Lessig, Lawrence. (2008). *Remix: Making Art and Commerce Thrive in the Hybrid Economy.* New York: Penguin.

Maher, Steve. (2007, June 5). Interviewed on *Frontline.* PBS. www.pbs.org/wgbh/pages/frontline/kidsonline/interviews/maher.html.

Nardi, Bonnie, and Vicki O'Day. (1999). *Information Ecologies: Teaching Technology with Heart.* Cambridge, MA: MIT Press.

November, Alan. (2007). "Space: The Final Frontier." *School Library Journal 53*(5), 44–45.

Selfe, Richard. (2005). *Sustainable Computer Environments: Cultures of Support in English Studies and Language Arts.* Cresskill, NJ: Hampton Press.

Valenti, Mark S. (2005, July/August). "Learning Space Design Precepts and Assumptions." *EDUCAUSE Review 40*(4), 40.

Warschauer, Mark. (2006). *Laptops and Literacy: Learning in the Wireless Classroom.* New York: Teachers College Press.

Chapter Four

Beach, Richard, Linda Clemens, and Kirsten Jamesen. (2009). "Digital Tools: Assessing Digital Communication and Providing Feedback to Student Writers." In Anne Burke and Roberta F. Hammett (Eds.), *Assessing New Literacies: Perspectives from the Classroom.* (157–76). New York: Peter Lang.

Bearne, Eve. (2009). "Assessing Multimodal Texts." In Anne Burke and Roberta F. Hammett (Eds.), *Assessing New Literacies: Perspectives from the Classroom.* (15–34). New York: Peter Lang.

Boardman, David. (2007). "Inside the Digital Classroom." In T. Newkirk and R. Kent (Eds.), *Teaching the Neglected "R": Rethinking Writing Instruction in Secondary Classrooms* (162–71). Portsmouth, NH: Heinemann.

Cambridge, Darren, Barbara Cambridge, and Kathleen Blake Yancey. (2009). *Electronic Portfolios 2.0: Emergent Research on Implementation and Impact.* Sterling, VA: Stylus.

Center for Media Literacy. (2008). *Literacy for the 21st Century: An Overview & Orientation Guide to Media Literacy Education* (2nd ed.). www.medialit.org/reading_room/article540.html.

Center for Social Media, School of Communication, American University. (n.d.). *Code of Best Practices in Fair Use for Media Literacy Education.* www.centerforsocialmedia.org/fair-use/best-practices/media-literacy.

Conference on College Composition and Communication. (2004). "Position Statement on Teaching, Learning, and Assessing in Digital Environments." www.ncte.org/cccc/resources/positions/digitalenvironments.

Eidman-Aadahl, Elyse. (2009, November 18). "Reimagining Literacy in the Digital Age." Opening remarks at the "Digital Is . . ." Convening, Philadelphia, PA.

Ericsson, Patricia Freitag, and Richard Haswell. (2006). *Machine Scoring of Student Essays: Truth and Consequences.* Logan: Utah State University Press.

Hamp-Lyons, Liz. (2004). "Review of Mark D. Shermis, Jill C. Burstein (Eds.) *Automated Essay Scoring.*" (Erlbaum, 2003). *Assessing Writing 9,* 262–65.

Herrington, Anne, Kevin Hodgson, and Charles Moran (Eds.). (2009). *Teaching the New Writing: Technology, Change, and Assessment in the 21st-Century Classroom.* New York: Teachers College Press; Berkeley, CA: National Writing Project (copublished).

Herrington, Anne, and Charles Moran. (2009). "Challenges for Writing Teachers: Evolving Technologies and Standardized Assessment." In Anne Herrington, Kevin Hodgson, and Charles Moran (Eds.), *Teaching the New Writing: Technology, Change, and Assessment in the 21st-Century Classroom* (1–17). New York: Teachers College Press; Berkeley, CA: National Writing Project (copublished).

Hillocks, George. (2002). *The Testing Trap: How State Writing Assessments Control Learning.* New York: Teachers College Press.

International Technology Education Association (ITEA). (1996). *Technology for All Americans: A Rationale and Structure for the Study of Technology.* www.iteaconnect.org/TAA/PDFs/Taa_RandS.pdf.

International Technology Education Association (ITEA). (2000). *Standards for Technological Literacy: Content for the Study of Technology.* www.iteaconnect.org/TAA/PDFs/Execsum.pdf.

International Society for Technology in Education (ISTE). (2007). *National Educational Technology Standards for Students* (2nd ed.). www.iste.org/source/Orders/isteProductDetail.cfm?product_code=nesbo2.

Knobel, Michele, and Colin Lankshear (Eds.). (2007). *A New Literacies Sampler.* New York: Peter Lang.

Michigan Department of Education. (2006). *High School Content Expectations: English Language Arts.* Lansing, MI.

Mid-continent Research for Education and Learning (McREL). (2009). *Content Knowledge Standards and Benchmark Database* (4th ed.). www.mcrel.org/standards-benchmarks/.

National Council of Teachers of English. (2008). "NCTE Framework for 21st Century Curriculum and Assessment." www.ncte.org/governance/21st centuryframework?source=gs.

Partnership for 21st Century Skills and the National Council of Teachers of English. (n.d.). "21st Century Skills Map: English." www.21stcenturyskills.org/documents/21st_century_skills_english_map.pdf.

Ribble, Mike, and Gerald Bailey. (2007). *Digital Citizenship in Schools*. Eugene, OR: International Society for Technology in Education.

Webb, Allen, and Robert Rozema. (2008). *Literature and the Web: Reading and Responding with New Technologies*. Portsmouth, NH: Heinemann.

Wilson, Maja. (2006). *Rethinking Rubrics in Writing Assessment*. Portsmouth, NH: Heinemann.

Yancey, Kathleen Blake. (2009). "Portfolios, Circulation, Ecology, and the Development of Literacy." In Dànielle Nicole DeVoss, Heidi McKee, and Richard (Dickie) Selfe (Eds.), *Technological Ecologies and Sustainability*. Computers and Composition Digital Press and Logan: Utah State University Press. Available at ccdigitalpress.org/tes/.

Chapter Five

Appalachian Technology in Education Consortium. (2007). *Technology in Schools: Evaluation of Kentucky's Student Technology Leadership Program (STLP)*. Available at www.e-archives.ky.gov/Pubs/Education/Research%20reports/ATECSTLP3.pdf.

Cochran-Smith, Marilyn, and Susan Lytle. (2009). *Inquiry as Stance: Practitioner Research in the Next Generation*. New York: Teachers College Press.

Consortium for School Networking. (2009). *Digital Leadership Divide*. www.cosn.org/Portals/7/docs/digital_leadership_divide.pdf.

Eidman-Aadahl, Elyse. (2009, November 18). "Reimagining Literacy in the Digital Age." Opening remarks at the "Digital Is . . ." Convening, Philadelphia, PA.

Elmore, Richard F., and Deanna Burney. (1997). *Improving Instruction Through Professional Development in New York City's Community District #2*. Policy Bulletin, Consortium for Policy Research in Education. Philadelphia: University of Pennsylvania. www.nctaf.org/documents/archive_investing-in-teacher-learning.pdf.

National Staff Development Council (NSDC). (2001). *NSDC's Standards for Staff Development* (revised). www.nsdc.org/standards/.

National Staff Development Council (NSDC). (2009). *Professional Learning in the Learning Profession: A Status Report on Teacher Development in the United States and Abroad*. www.nsdc.org/news/NSDCstudy2009.pdf.

National Writing Project. (2008). "Dakota Writing Project Provides a Different Kind of Technology Hotline for Teachers." www.nwp.org/cs/public/print/resource/2562.

National Writing Project and Carl Nagin. (2006). *Because Writing Matters: Improving Student Writing in Our Schools* (Rev. ed.). San Francisco: Jossey-Bass.

Nielsen, Lisa. (2008). "5 Things You Can Do to Begin Developing Your Personal Learning Network." The Innovative Educator, October 12, 2008. theinnovativeeducator .blogspot.com/2008/04/5-things-you-can-do-to-begin-developing.html.

Richardson, Will. (2010). "The PD Problem." Weblogg-ed, March 14, 2010. weblogg-ed.com/category/professional-development/.

Selfe, Richard. (2003). *Techno-Pedagogical Explorations: Toward Sustainable Technology-Rich Instruction.* In Pamela Takayoshi and Brian Huot (Eds.), *Teaching Writing with Computers: An Introduction.* (17–32). Boston: Houghton Mifflin.

Selfe, Richard. (2004). *Sustainable Computer Environments: Cultures of Support in English Studies and Language Arts.* Cresskill, NJ: Hampton Press.

Swenson, Janet, Robert Rozema, Carl A. Young, Ewa McGrail, and Phyllis Whitin. (2005). "Beliefs About Technology and the Preparation of English Teachers: Beginning the Conversation." *Contemporary Issues in Technology and Teacher Education* [Online journal] 5(3/4). Available at www.citejournal.org/vol5/iss3/ languagearts/article1.cfm.

Afterword

Collins, Allan, and Richard Halverson. (2009). *Rethinking Education in the Age of Technology.* New York: Teachers College Press.

Cuban, Larry. (2001). *Oversold and Underused: Computers in the Classroom.* Cambridge, MA: Harvard University Press.

McKee, Heidi A., and Dànielle Nicole DeVoss. (2007). *Digital Writing Research.* Cresskill, NJ: Hampton Press.

National Writing Project and Carl Nagin. (2006). *Because Writing Matters: Improving Student Writing in Our Schools* (Rev. ed.). San Francisco: Jossey-Bass.

Smith, Fran. (2007, April). *My School, Meet MySpace: Social Networking at School.* Edutopia. Retrieved December 18, 2009, from www.edutopia.org/my-school-meet-myspace#.

Wiggins, Grant P., and Jay McTighe. (2005). *Understanding by Design* (2nd ed.). New York: Prentice Hall.

BIBLIOGRAPHY

Appalachian Technology in Education Consortium. (2007). *Technology in Schools: Evaluation of Kentucky's Student Technology Leadership Program (STLP).* Available at www.e-archives.ky.gov/Pubs/Education/Research%20reports/ATECSTLP3.pdf.

Beach, Richard, Chris Anson, Lee-Ann Kastman Breuch, and Thom Swiss. (2008). *Teaching Writing Using Blogs, Wikis, and Other Digital Tools.* Norwood, MA: Christopher-Gordon.

Beach, Richard, Linda Clemens, and Kirsten Jamsen. (2009). "Digital Tools: Assessing Digital Communication and Providing Feedback to Student Writers." In Anne Burke and Roberta F. Hammett (Eds.), *Assessing New Literacies: Perspectives from the Classroom* (157–76). New York: Peter Lang.

Bearne, Eve. (2009). "Assessing Multimodal Texts." In Anne Burke and Roberta F. Hammett (Eds.), *Assessing New Literacies: Perspectives from the Classroom* (15–34). New York: Peter Lang.

Belden Russonello & Stewart. (2007). *The 2007 Survey on Teaching Writing— American Public Opinion on the Importance of Writing in Schools.* Conducted for the National Writing Project. Washington, DC: Belden Russonello & Stewart.

Besser, Howard. (2001). "The Next Digital Divides." *Teaching to Change LA (TCLA) 1*(2). Retrieved October 17, 2008, from tcla.gseis.ucla.edu/divide/politics/besser.html.

Boardman, David. (2007). "Inside the Digital Classroom." In T. Newkirk and R. Kent (Eds.), *Teaching the Neglected "R": Rethinking Writing Instruction in Secondary Classrooms* (162–171). Portsmouth, NH: Heinemann.

Brown, Malcolm. (2005, July/August). "Learning Space Design Theory and Practice." *EDUCAUSE Review 40*(4), 30.

Cambridge, Darren, Barbara Cambridge, and Kathleen Blake Yancey. (2009). *Electronic Portfolios 2.0: Emergent Research on Implementation and Impact.* Sterling, VA: Stylus.

Center for Digital Storytelling. (n.d.). Available at storycenter.org/index1.html.

Center for Media Literacy. (2008). *Literacy for the 21st Century: An Overview & Orientation Guide to Media Literacy Education* (2nd ed.). www.medialit.org/reading_room/article540.html.

Center for Social Media, School of Communication, American University. (n.d.). *Code of Best Practices in Fair Use for Media Literacy Education*. www.centerforsocialmedia.org/fair-use/best-practices/media-literacy.

Childers, Pamela. (2004). "Interacting with Computer Technology in Secondary Schools." *Computers and Composition 20*(4), 473–80.

Chism, Nancy Van Note. (2006). "Challenging Traditional Assumptions and Rethinking Learning Spaces." Chapter 2 in Diana Oblinger, *Learning Spaces*. Educause. Retrieved January 28, 2009, from www.educause.edu/LearningSpacesch2.

Cochran-Smith, Marilyn, and Susan Lytle. (2009). *Inquiry as Stance: Practitioner Research in the Next Generation*. New York: Teachers College Press.

Collins, Allan, and Richard Halverson. (2009). *Rethinking Education in the Age of Technology.* New York: Teachers College Press.

Common Sense Media. (n.d.). Digital Literacy and Citizenship Curriculum. Available at www.commonsensemedia.org/how-be-common-sense-school2.

Conference on College Composition and Communication. (2004). "Position Statement on Teaching, Learning, and Assessing in Digital Environments." Available at www.ncte.org/cccc/resources/positions/digitalenvironments.

Consortium for School Networking. (2009). *Digital Leadership Divide.* Available at www.cosn.org/Portals/7/docs/digital_leadership_divide.pdf.

Copyright-Friendly and *Copyleft* Images and Sound (Mostly!) for Use in Media Projects and Web Pages, Blogs, Wikis, etc. (n.d.). Available at copyrightfriendly.wikispaces.com/.

Cuban, Larry. (1986). *Teachers and Machines: The Classroom Use of Technology Since 1920*. New York: Teachers College Press.

Cuban, Larry. (2001). *Oversold and Underused: Computers in the Classroom.* Cambridge, MA: Harvard University Press.

DeVoss, Dànielle Nicole, and Dickie Selfe. (2002). "Encouraging and Supporting Electronic Communication Across the Curriculum Through a University and K–12 Partnership." *Computers and Composition 19*(4), 435–51.

Eidman-Aadahl, Elyse. (2009, November 18). "Reimagining Literacy in the Digital Age." Opening remarks at the "Digital Is . . ." Convening, Philadelphia, PA

Elbow, Peter. (1998a). *Writing Without Teachers* (2nd ed.). New York: Oxford University Press.

Elbow, Peter. (1998b). *Writing with Power* (2nd ed.). New York: Oxford University Press.

Elmore, Richard F., and Deanna Burney. (1997). *Improving Instruction Through Professional Development in New York City's Community District #2*. Policy Bulletin,

Consortium for Policy Research in Education. Philadelphia: University of Pennsylvania. Available at www.nctaf.org/documents/archive_investing-in-teacher-learning.pdf.

Ericsson, Patricia Freitag, and Richard Haswell. (2006). *Machine Scoring of Student Essays: Truth and Consequences.* Logan: Utah State University Press.

Fisch, Karl, and Scott McLeod. (2007). *Did You Know?: Shift Happens.* Retrieved December 21, 2008, from www.youtube.com/watch?v=pMcfrLYDm2U &feature=related.

Global Kids, the Goodplay Project at Harvard University's Project Zero, and Common Sense Media. (2009). *A Meeting of the Minds: Cross-Generational Dialogues on the Ethics of Digital Life.* Available at www.globalkids.org/meetingofminds.pdf.

Graham, Steve, Charles A. MacArthur, and Jill Fitzgerald. (2007). *Best Practices in Writing Instruction.* New York: Guilford Press.

Graham, Steve, and Dolores Perin. (2007). *Writing Next: Effective Strategies to Improve Writing of Adolescents in Middle and High Schools—A Report to Carnegie Corporation of New York.* Washington, DC: Alliance for Excellent Education. Retrieved September 13, 2009, from www.all4ed.org/files/WritingNext.pdf.

Haas, Angela. (2008). "What American Indians Can Tell Us About Memoria, Hypertext, Visual and Digital Rhetoric, and Technical Communication." Unpublished doctoral dissertation. Michigan State University, East Lansing, MI.

Hamp-Lyons, Liz. (2004). "Review of Mark D. Shermis, Jill C. Burstein (Eds.), *Automated Essay Scoring.*" (Erlbaum, 2003). *Assessing Writing 9,* 262–65.

Hargadon, Steve. (2007). "A 14-year-old Talks Educational Technology." *K–12 Educational Technology,* October 19, 2007. Available at www.stevehargadon.com/2007/10/14-year-old-talks-educational.html.

Herrington, Anne, Kevin Hodgson, and Charles Moran (Eds.). (2009). *Teaching the New Writing: Technology, Change, and Assessment in the 21st-Century Classroom.* New York: Teachers College Press; Berkeley, CA: National Writing Project (copublished).

Herrington, Anne, and Charles Moran. 2009. "Challenges for Writing Teachers: Evolving Technologies and Standardized Assessment." In Anne Herrington, Kevin Hodgson, and Charles Moran (Eds.), *Teaching the New Writing: Technology, Change, and Assessment in the 21st-Century Classroom* (1–17). New York: Teachers College Press; Berkeley, CA: National Writing Project (copublished).

Hicks, Troy. (2009). *The Digital Writing Workshop.* Portsmouth, NH: Heinemann.

Hillocks, George. (2002). *The Testing Trap: How State Writing Assessments Control Learning.* New York: Teachers College Press.

Hunt, Bud. (2005). Sample Blog Acceptable Use Policy. Available at www.budtheteacher .com/wiki/index.php?title=Sample_Blog_Acceptable_Use_Policy.

International Society for Technology in Education (ISTE). (n.d.). *National Educational Technology Standards (NETS) for Students 2007*. Retrieved May 19, 2009, from www.iste.org/AM/ Template.cfm?Section=NETS.

International Society for Technology in Education (ISTE). 2007. *National Educational Technology Standards for Students* (2nd ed.). Available at www.iste.org/source/Orders/isteProductDetail.cfm?product_code=nesbo2.

International Technology Education Association (ITEA). (1996). *Technology for All Americans: A Rationale and Structure for the Study of Technology*. Available at www.iteaconnect.org/TAA/PDFs/Taa_RandS.pdf.

International Technology Education Association (ITEA). (2000). *Standards for Technological Literacy: Content for the Study of Technology*. Available at www.iteaconnect.org/TAA/PDFs/Execsum.pdf.

Ito, Mizuko, Heather Horst, Matteo Bittani, danah boyd, Becky Herr-Stephenson, Patricia G. Lange, C. J. Pascoe, and Laura Robinson. (2008). *Living and Learning with New Media: Summary of Findings from the Digital Youth Project*. John D. and Catherine T. MacArthur Foundation Reports on Digital Media and Learning. Available at digitalyouth.ischool.berkeley.edu/files/report/digitalyouth-WhitePaper.pdf.

James, Carrie. (2009). *Young People, Ethics, and the New Digital Media*. John D. and Catherine T. MacArthur Foundation. Available at mitpress.mit.edu/catalog/item/default.asp?ttype=2&tid=12009&mode=toc.

Jenkins, Henry, Kate Clinton, Ravi Purushotma, Alice J. Robinson, and Margaret Weigel. (2006). *Confronting the Challenges of Participatory Culture: Media Education for the 21st Century*. John D. and Catherine T. MacArthur Foundation occasional paper on digital media and learning. Available at digitallearning.macfound.org/site/c.enJLKQNlFiG/b.2108773/apps/nl/content2.asp?content_id={CD911571–0240–4714-A93B-1D0C07C7B6C1}&notoc=1.

Johnson, Chris, and Cyprien Lomas. (2005, July/August). "Design of the Learning Space: Learning and Design Principles." *EDUCAUSE Review 40*(4), 16–28.

Joseph, Chris. (2005). State of the Art. trAce Online Writing Centre. Retrieved August 30, 2008, from tracearchive.ntu.ac.uk/Process/index.cfm?article=131.

Knobel, Michele, and Colin Lankshear (Eds.). (2007). *A New Literacies Sampler*. New York: Peter Lang.

Lankshear, Colin, and Michele Knobel. (2006). *New Literacies: Everyday Practices and Classroom Learning* (2nd ed.). Maidenhead, NY: Open University Press.

Lee, Akili. (2007). "Designing a Social Networking Site." Retrieved October 9, 2009, from spotlight.macfound.org/blog/entry/akili_lee_designing_social_networking/.

Lenhart, Amanda, Sousan Arafeh, Aaron Smith, and Alexandra Rankin Macgill. (2008, April). *Writing, Technology and Teens*. Pew Internet & American Life Project, with the National Commission on Writing. Available at

www.pcwinternet .org/~/media//Files/Reports/2008/PIP_Writing_Report_
FINAL3.pdf.pdf.

Lessig, Lawrence. (2005). *Free Culture: The Nature and Future of Creativity*. New York: Penguin.

Lessig, Lawrence. (2008). *Remix: Making Art and Commerce Thrive in the Hybrid Economy*. New York: Penguin.

Maher, Steve. (2007, June 5). Interviewed on *Frontline*. PBS. Available at www.pbs.org/wgbh/pages/frontline/kidsonline/interviews/maher.html.

McKee, Heidi A., and Dànielle Nicole DeVoss. (2007). *Digital Writing Research*. Cresskill, NJ: Hampton Press.

Mid-continent Research for Education and Learning (McREL). (2009). *Content Knowledge Standards and Benchmark Database* (4th ed.). Available at www.mcrel.org/standards-benchmarks/.

Mishra, Punya, and Matthew J. Koehler. (n.d.). TPACK Wiki. Available at www.tpack.org/tpck/index.php?title=Main_Page.

Mishra, Punya, and Matthew J. Koehler. (2006). "Technological Pedagogical Content Knowledge: A New Framework for Teacher Knowledge." *Teachers College Record 108*(6), 1017–54.

Nardi, Bonnie, and Vicki L. O'Day. (1999). *Information Ecologies: Teaching Technology with Heart*. Cambridge, MA: MIT Press.

National Commission on Writing for America's Families, Schools, and Colleges. (2003). *The Neglected "R": The Need for a Writing Revolution*. Retrieved December 21, 2008, from www.writingcommission.org/prod_downloads/writingcom/writing-ticket-to-work.pdf.

National Commission on Writing for America's Families, Schools, and Colleges. (2004). *Writing: A Ticket to Work . . . Or a Ticket Out: A Survey of Business Leaders*. Retrieved July 17, 2010, from www.collegeboard.com/prod_downloads/writingcom/writing-ticket-to-work.pdf.

National Council of Teachers of English. (2007). *21st Century Literacies: A Policy Research Brief Produced by the National Council of Teachers of English*. Retrieved December 21, 2008, from www.ncte.org/library/NCTEFiles/Resources/PolicyResearch/21stCenturyResearchBrief.pdf.

National Council of Teachers of English. (2008). "NCTE Framework for 21st Century Curriculum and Assessment." Available at www.ncte.org/governance/21stcenturyframework?source=gs.

National Council of Teachers of English. (2008). *Writing Now: A Policy Research Brief Produced by the National Council of Teachers of English*. Retrieved December 21, 2008, from www.ncte.org/library/NCTEFiles/Resources/PolicyResearch/WrtgResearchBrief.pdf.

National Staff Development Council. (2001). *NSDC's Standards for Staff Development* (Rev. ed.). Available at www.nsdc.org/standards/.

National Staff Development Council. (2009). *Professional Learning in the Learning Profession: A Status Report on Teacher Development in the United States and Abroad*. Available at www.nsdc.org/news/NSDCstudy2009.pdf.

National Writing Project. (2008). "Dakota Writing Project Provides a Different Kind of Technology Hotline for Teachers." Available at www.nwp.org/cs/public/print/resource/2562.

National Writing Project and Carl Nagin. 2006. *Because Writing Matters: Improving Student Writing in Our Schools* (Rev. ed.). San Francisco: Jossey-Bass.

Nielsen, Lisa. (2008). "5 Things You Can Do to Begin Developing Your Personal Learning Network." The Innovative Educator, October 12, 2008. Available at theinnovativeeducator.blogspot.com/2008/04/5-things-you-can-do-to-begin-developing.html.

November, Alan. (2007). "Space: The Final Frontier." *School Library Journal* 53(5), 44–45.

Ohler, Jason. (2009). "Orchestrating the Digital Collage." *Educational Leadership* 66(4), 8–13.

Oppenheimer, Todd. (2003). *The Flickering Mind: The False Promise of Technology in the Classroom, and How Learning Can Be Saved*. New York: Random House.

Palmquist, Mike. (2003). "A Brief History of Computer Support for Writing Centers and Writing-Across-The-Curriculum Programs." *Computers and Composition 20*(4), 395–413.

Partnership for 21st Century Skills and the National Council of Teachers of English. (n.d.). *21st Century Skills Map: English.* Retrieved May 19, 2009, from www.21stcenturyskills.org/documents/21st_century_skills_english_map.pdf.

Porter, Bernajean. (2005). *DigiTales: The Art of Telling Digital Stories*. Denver, CO: bjpconsulting. Available at www.digitales.us/.

Prabhu, M. (2008, October 21). "'Digital Disconnect' Divides Kids, Educators." *eSchool News*. Retrieved December 21, 2008, from www.eschoolnews.com/news/top-news/ index.cfm?i=55665.

Prensky, Marc. (2001, October). *Digital Natives, Digital Immigrants—Part1.* Retrieved December 21, 2008, from www.marcprensky.com/writing/Prensky%20-%20Digital%20Natives,%20Digital%20Immigrants%20-%20Part1.pdf.

Ribble, Mike, and Gerald Bailey. (2007). *Digital Citizenship in Schools*. Eugene, OR: International Society for Technology in Education.

Richardson, Will. (2010). "The PD Problem." Weblogg-ed, March 14, 2010. Available at weblogg-ed.com/category/professional-development/.

Selber, Stuart. (2004a). *Multiliteracies for a Digital Age*. Carbondale: Southern Illinois University Press.

Selber, Stuart. (2004b). "Technological Dramas: A Metadiscourse Heuristic for Critical Literacy." *Computers and Composition 21*, 171–95

Selfe, Richard. (2003). "Techno-Pedagogical Explorations: Toward Sustainable Technology-Rich Instruction." In Pamela Takayoshi and Brian Huot (Eds.), *Teaching Writing with Computers: An Introduction* (17–32). Boston: Houghton Mifflin.

Selfe, Richard. (2004). *Sustainable Computer Environments: Cultures of Support in English Studies and Language Arts*. Cresskill, NJ: Hampton Press.

Smith, Fran. (2007, April). *My School, Meet MySpace: Social Networking at School.* Edutopia. Retrieved December 18, 2009, from www.edutopia.org/my-school-meet-myspace#.

Swenson, Janet, Robert Rozema, Carl A. Young, Ewa McGrail, and Phyllis Whitin. (2005). "Beliefs About Technology and the Preparation of English Teachers: Beginning the Conversation." *Contemporary Issues in Technology and Teacher Education* [Online journal] *5*(3/4). Available at www.citejournal.org/vol5/iss3/languagearts/article1.cfm.

Swenson, Janet, Carl A. Young, Ewa McGrail, Robert Rozema, and Phyllis Whitin. (2005). "Extending the Conversation: New Technologies, New Literacies, and English Education." *English Education 38*(4), 351–69.

Vaidhyanathan, Siva. (2008, September 19). "Generational Myth: Not All Young People Are Tech-Savvy." *Chronicle of Higher Education: Chronicle Review.* Retrieved October 12, 2008, from chronicle.com/free/v55/i04/04b00701.htm?utm_source=cr&utm_medium=en.

Valenti, Mark S. (2005, July/August). "Learning Space Design Precepts and Assumptions." *EDUCAUSE Review 40*(4), 40.

Warschauer, Mark. (2006). *Laptops and Literacy: Learning in the Wireless Classroom.* New York: Teachers College Press.

Webb, Allen, and Robert Rozema. (2008). *Literature and the Web: Reading and Responding with New Technologies.* Portsmouth, NH: Heinemann.

Wesch, Michael. (2007). *A Vision of Students Today.* Retrieved December 21, 2008, from www.youtube.com/watch?v=dGCJ46vyR9o.

Writing in Digital Environments (WIDE) Research Collective. (2005). "Why Teach 'Digital Writing'?" *Kairos: A Journal of Rhetoric, Technology, and Pedagogy 10*(1). Retrieved December 21, 2008, from english.ttu.edu/Kairos/10.1/coverWeb/wide/index.html.

Wiggins, Grant P., and Jay McTighe. (2005). *Understanding by Design* (2nd ed.). New York: Prentice Hall.

Wilson, Maja. (2006). *Rethinking Rubrics in Writing Assessment.* Portsmouth, NH: Heinemann.

Yancey, Kathleen Blake. (2009). "Portfolios, Circulation, Ecology, and the Development of Literacy." In Dànielle Nicole DeVoss, Heidi McKee, and Richard (Dickie) Selfe (Eds.), *Technological Ecologies and Sustainability.* Computers and Composition Digital Press and Logan: Utah State University Press. Available at: ccdigitalpress.org/tes/.

Bread Loaf Teacher Network

www.middlebury.edu/

The Bread Loaf Teacher Network is a network of teachers connected to the Bread Loaf School of English at Middlebury College and supported by BreadNet, one of the first electronic teacher networks in the nation.

Bud the Teacher

budtheteacher.com

Bud the Teacher is the blog of Bud Hunt, an instructional technologist for the St. Vrain Valley School District in northern Colorado and teacher-consultant for the Colorado State University Writing Project.

Center for Advanced Technology in Education

cate2.uoregon.edu:8020

The Center for Advanced Technology in Education, which houses the Oregon Writing Project, is a research and outreach center at the College of Education at the University of Oregon, dedicated to investigating and promoting the use of advanced technology in education.

Center for Digital Storytelling

storycenter.org

The Center for Digital Storytelling is an international nonprofit training, project development, and research organization dedicated to assisting people in using digital media to tell meaningful stories from their lives.

Center for Media Literacy

www.medialit.org

The Center for Media Literacy provides leadership, public education, professional development, and educational resources nationally to promote and support media literacy education.

Center for Research on Writing and Communication Technologies

www.colostate.edu/Depts/CROWACT

The Center for Research on Writing and Communication Technologies supports interdisciplinary teams at the Colorado State University in conducting research that explores the impact of communication technologies on instructional and professional settings.

Center for Social Media

www.centerforsocialmedia.org

The Center for Social Media of the American University School of Communication investigates, showcases, and sets standards for socially engaged media making.

Children's Internet Protection Act (CIPA)

www.fcc.gov.akadns.net/cgb/consumerfacts/cipa.html

The Children's Internet Protection Act is a United States federal law enacted by Congress to address concerns about access to offensive content over the Internet on school and library computers.

Classroom 2.0 Social Network

classroom20.com

Classroom20.com is a social network for those interested in Web 2.0 and collaborative technologies in education.

Code of Best Practices in Fair Use for Media Literacy Education

www.centerforsocialmedia.org/fair-use/related-materials/codes/
code-best-practices-fair-use-media-literacy-education
The *Code of Best Practices* helps educators using media literacy concepts and
techniques to interpret the copyright doctrine of fair use.

Also available at the Temple University Media Education Lab (this Web site
also has case study videos and lesson plans):
www.mediaeducationlab.com/code-best-practices-fair-use-media-literacy-
education
Also available at the National Council of Teachers of English: www.ncte.org/
positions/statements/fairusemedialiteracy

Common Sense Media

www.commonsensemedia.org
Common Sense Media is a nonpartisan, not-for-profit organization focused
on providing families and educators with high-quality information about
youth media as well as reviews of popular games, Web sites, and media
products.

www.commonsensemedia.org/digital-citizenship/6-8
Digital Citizenship in a Connected Culture is a Common Sense Media curriculum designed to empower responsible and engaged digital citizens;
designed for students, grades six to eight, and their families.

Consortium for School Networking (CoSN)

www.cosn.org
The Consortium for School Networking is a professional association for
K–12 school district technology leaders to use technology strategically
to improve teaching and learning.

Contemporary Issues in Technology and Teacher Education (CITE)

CITEJournal.org
CITE Journal is a peer-reviewed online journal published by the Society
for Information Technology & Teacher Education (SITE).

Creative Commons

creativecommons.org

Creative Commons is a nonprofit corporation dedicated to making it easier for people to share and build upon the work of others, consistent with the rules of copyright.

Did You Know?/Shift Happens Presentation Wiki

shifthappens.wikispaces.com

The Did You Know?/Shift Happens Presentation wiki gives background about the *Did You Know?* presentation and provides resources addressing the shifts that are occurring in education, K–12 and higher.

Digital Arts Alliance, Pearson Foundation

www.digitalartsalliance.org

The Digital Arts Alliance of the Pearson Foundation delivers educational experiences by providing fully funded and fully equipped digital arts programs to middle schools, high schools, and community centers across the United States.

Digital Citizenship

www.digitalcitizenship.net

Digital Citizenship is a teaching tool that helps teachers, technology leaders, and parents to understand what students, children, and technology users should know to use technology appropriately.

DigiTales: The Art of Writing Digital Stories

www.digitales.us

DigiTales provides ideas, resources, and inspiration for families, individuals, schools, organizations, corporations, and churches to merge the art of storytelling with the skills of using digital tools.

Digital Ethnography Blog

mediatedcultures.net

This is group blog led by Dr. Michael Wesch dedicated to exploring and extending the possibilities of digital ethnography.

Digital Writing Wiki

digitalwriting.pbworks.com

The Digital Writing Wiki is designed to support the book *Teaching Writing Using Blogs, Wikis, and Other Digital Tools*.

Digital Writing Workshop Wiki

digitalwritingworkshop.wikispaces.com/

The Digital Writing Workshop wiki is a companion site to the book *The Digital Writing Workshop*.

Digital Youth Network

iremix.org

The Digital Youth Network is a hybrid digital literacy program—connecting classroom, after-school, and home activities—that creates opportunities for youth to engage in learning environments that span both school and out-of-school contexts.

Digital Youth Project

digitalyouth.ischool.berkeley.edu

The Digital Youth Project is a study carried out by researchers at the University of Southern California (USC) and University of California, Berkeley, that explores how kids use digital media in their everyday lives.

EdTechLIVE

www.edtechlive.com

EdTechLIVE is a Webcast interview series by Steve Hargadon of Classroom 2.0 focused on K–12 educational technology.

EdTechTalk

www.edtechtalk.com

EdTechTalk is a community of educators using Webcasting and other related technology to discuss and learn about the uses of educational technology.

Educause

www.educause.edu

Educause is a nonprofit association whose mission is to advance higher education by promoting the intelligent use of information technology.

Enhancing Education Through Technology

www.ed.gov/programs/edtech

Enhancing Education Through Technology is a program of the U.S. Department of Education created to improve student achievement through the use of technology in elementary and secondary schools.

E-Rate

www.fcc.gov/learnnet

E-Rate is a program of the U.S. Federal Communications Commission that assists in connecting public school classrooms and libraries to modern telecommunication networks.

Everybody Writes

www.everybodywrites.org.uk

Everybody Writes offers classroom teachers innovative ideas and practical resources to get primary pupils and secondary students excited about writing.

Frontline's "Growing Up Online"

www.pbs.org/wgbh/pages/frontline/kidsonline

Frontline's "Growing Up Online" investigates how the Internet is transforming the experience of childhood.

Global Kids' Online Leadership Program

www.globalkids.org

Global Kids' Online Leadership Program integrates a youth development approach and international and public policy issues into youth media programs that build digital literacy, foster substantive online dialogues, develop resources for educators, and promote civic participation.

GoodPlay Project

www.goodworkproject.org/research/digital.htm

The GoodPlay Project explores the ethical character of young people's activities in the new digital media by seeking to understand how they conceptualize their participation in virtual worlds and the ethical considerations that guide their conduct.

High Tech High Network

www.hightechhigh.org

High Tech High began as a charter high school in San Diego and now includes a network of K–12 schools, a teacher certification program, and a Graduate School of Education.

Holocaust Educators Network

www.holocausteducators.org

The Holocaust Educators Network provides a forum for educators interested in studying and teaching the Holocaust using an inquiry-based approach to engage students with difficult material and show how writing and dialogue can help move students from shock and denial to empathy and action.

I Dig Science

olpglobalkids.org/virtual_worlds/i_dig_science

I Dig Science is a project of Global Kids with the Field Museum of Chicago. Starting in 2008, groups of high schoolers in New York City and Chicago have gone into the virtual world to learn about science, evolution, and biology, as well as the complex social and cultural issues of particular countries.

The Innovative Educator

theinnovativeeducator.blogspot.com

The Innovative Educator is a blog maintained by Lisa Nielsen to share information, ideas, and resources with other educators as well as begin to grow a community interested in educating innovatively.

Inter/National Coalition for Electronic Portfolio Research

ncepr.org

The Inter/National Coalition for Electronic Portfolio Research studies the impact of electronic portfolio use on student learning and educational outcomes.

International Reading Association

www.reading.org

The International Reading Association is a nonprofit, global network of individuals and institutions that supports literacy professionals through a wide range of resources, advocacy efforts, volunteerism, and professional development activities.

International Society for Technology in Education

www.iste.org

The International Society for Technology in Education is a resource for professional development, knowledge generation, advocacy, and leadership for innovation.

International Technology Education Association (ITEA)

www.iteaconnect.org

The International Technology Education Association is a professional organization for technology, innovation, design, and engineering educators that promotes technological literacy.

Kentucky's Commonwealth Accountability Testing System

www.education.ky.gov/KDE/Administrative+Resources/Testing+and+Reporting+/Kentucky+School+Testing+System/

This Web site contains information and resources related to the Kentucky Department of Education School Testing System.

Kevin's Meandering Mind

dogtrax.edublogs.org

Kevin's Meandering Mind is a blog maintained by educator Kevin Hodgson from Southampton, Massachusetts.

Maine Learning Technology Initiative

www.maine.gov/mlti

The Maine Learning Technology Initiative provides professional development and twenty-first-century tools to secondary education teachers and
students in the state of Maine.

Media Education Lab, Temple University

mediaeducationlab.com

The mission of the Media Education Lab at Temple University is to improve
media literacy education through scholarship and community service.

Mid-continent Research for Education and Learning (McREL)

www.mcrel.org

McREL is a private nonprofit corporation dedicated to making a difference
in public education by drawing upon the best of education research to
translate what works into innovations and results.

National Assessment of Educational Progress (NAEP)

nces.ed.gov/nationsreportcard

The National Assessment of Educational Progress conducts national
assessments in mathematics, reading, science, writing, the arts, civics, eco-
nomics, geography, and United States history for the U.S. Department of
Education.

National Commission on Teaching and America's Future

www.nctaf.org

The National Commission on Teaching and America's Future is focused on
closing the student achievement gap by calling on policymakers and
education leaders to provide every child in America with twenty-first-
century teaching.

National Commission on Writing

www.writingcommission.org

The National Commission on Writing for America's Families, Schools, and
Colleges was established by the College Board to focus national attention on the teaching and learning of writing.

National Council of Teachers of English (NCTE)

www.ncte.org

The National Council of Teachers of English is a professional association of educators in English studies, literacy, and language arts.

NCTE's Conference on College Composition and Communication (CCCC)

www.ncte.org/cccc

The Conference on College Composition and Communication of the National Council of Teachers of English supports and promotes the teaching and study of college composition and communication and is an advocate for language and literacy education nationally and internationally.

National Staff Development Council's (NSDC) Standards for Professional Development

www.nsdc.org/standards

The National Staff Development Council is a nonprofit professional organization that organizes adults into learning communities to support adult learning and collaboration.

National Writing Project (NWP)

www.nwp.org

The National Writing Project is a network of sites anchored at colleges and universities, serving teachers across disciplines and at all levels, that focuses the knowledge, expertise, and leadership of our nation's educators on sustained efforts to improve writing and learning for all learners.

NWP's Digital Is

digitalis.nwp.org

The National Writing Project's Digital Is Web site is a teaching-focused knowledge base exploring the art and craft of writing, the teaching and learning of writing, along with provocations that push on our thinking as educators and learners in the digital age.

NWP's E-Anthology

www.nwp.org/cs/public/print/programs/ea

The National Writing Project's E-Anthology is a national online forum dedicated to supporting invitational summer institutes, providing participants a safe online space to publish their writing and reflections during the institute.

NWP's Technology Initiative

www.nwp.org/cs/public/print/programs/ti

The National Writing Project's Technology Initiative provides opportunities for Writing Project sites to better understand the impact of new digital tools and information and communication technology on the teaching of writing and literacy learning.

NWP's Technology Liaisons Network

www.nwp.org/cs/public/print/programs/tln

The National Writing Project's Technology Liaisons Network provides opportunities for local Writing Project sites and leaders to consider the impact technology is having on the teaching and learning of writing and on the general work of Writing Project sites.

NeverEndingSearch

blog.schoollibraryjournal.com/neverendingsearch

NeverEndingSearch is a blog by Joyce Valenza, a teacher-librarian at Springfield Township High School and a technology writer at the *School Library Journal*.

New Media Literacies

newmedialiteracies.org

New Media Literacies is a research initiative based within the USC's Annenberg School for Communication that explores how we might best equip young people with the social skills and cultural competencies required to become full participants in the emergent media landscape.

New Tech Network

www.newtechfoundation.org

The New Tech Network works nationally with schools, districts, and communities to develop innovative high schools.

New Youth City Learning Network

newyouthcity.net

The New Youth City Learning Network is a group of cultural institutions working together to create and connect learning opportunities for local middle and high school–aged youth in New York.

One Laptop Per Child

www.laptop.org

One Laptop Per Child creates educational opportunities for the world's poorest children by providing each child with a rugged, low-cost, low-power, connected laptop with content and software designed for collaborative, joyful, self-empowered learning.

Pacific Bell/UCLA Initiative for 21st Century Literacy

www.newliteracies.gseis.ucla.edu

The Pacific Bell/UCLA Initiative for 21st Century Literacy strives to provide a constellation of twenty-first-century literacy skills—including cultural, information, and media literacy—that provides students, teachers, librarians, and all citizens with critical tools needed to flourish today and tomorrow.

Partnership for 21st Century Skills

www.21stcenturyskills.org

The Partnership for 21st Century Skills aids schools, districts, and states in implementing the infusion of twenty-first-century technology skills into education, and provides tools and resources.

Pew Internet & American Life Project

www.pewinternet.org

The Pew Internet & American Life Project produces reports that explore the impact of the internet on families, communities, work and home, daily life, education, health care, and civic and political life.

Project Tomorrow

www.tomorrow.org

Project Tomorrow supports the innovative uses of science, math, and technology resources in K–12 schools and communities so that students will develop the critical-thinking, problem-solving, and creativity skills needed to compete and thrive in the twenty-first century.

Public Domain Sherpa

www.publicdomainsherpa.com

The Public Domain Sherpa site provides information on finding and using public domain material in the United States.

Science Leadership Academy (SLA)

www.scienceleadership.org

The Science Leadership Academy is a partnership high school between the School District of Philadelphia and The Franklin Institute. SLA is an inquiry-driven, project-based high school focused on twenty-first-century learning.

Springfield Township Virtual Library

springfieldlibrary.wikispaces.com

The Springfield Township Virtual Library is a wiki-based virtual library for the Springfield Township High School, Pennsylvania, maintained by librarian Joyce Valenza.

State of the Art

www.chrisjoseph.org

State of the Art is a blog by digital writer and artist Chris Joseph.

Student Technology Leadership Program, Kentucky Department of Education

www.education.ky.gov/KDE/Instructional+Resources/Technology/ Student+Initiatives/STLP+Student+Technology+Leadership+Program

The Student Technology Leadership Program is a Kentucky Department of Education project-based learning program that empowers students in all grade levels to use technology to learn and achieve.

Teachers Teaching Teachers

teachersteachingteachers.org

Through a weekly interactive Webcast hosted by EdTechTalk, New York City Writing Project teachers bring together other teachers from across the country and the globe to discuss issues of classroom practice with new digital technology and to think through shared curriculum projects.

TPACK (Technological Pedagogical Content Knowledge)

www.tpck.org

TPACK attempts to capture some of the essential qualities of knowledge required by teachers to integrate technology in their teaching, while addressing the complex, multifaceted, and situated nature of teacher knowledge.

A Vision of Students Today

www.youtube.com/watch?v=dGCJ46vyR9o&feature=player_embedded

A Vision of Students Today is a short video directed by Dr. Michael Wesch summarizing some of the most important characteristics of students today—how they learn; what they need to learn; their goals, hopes, and dreams.

Web 2.0 . . . The Machine Is Us/ing Us

www.youtube.com/watch?v=NLlGopyXT_g&feature=channel

Web 2.0 . . . The Machine is Us/ing Us is a short video directed by Dr. Michael Wesch that speaks to the implications of digital technologies for our lives.

Weblogg-ed

www.weblogg-ed.com

Weblogg-ed is a blog maintained by Will Richardson, the "Learner in Chief" at Connective Learning, a consultancy service specializing in assisting educators in understanding and implementing the latest workplace and leadership practices.

WIDE (Writing in Digital Environments) Research Center

wide.msu.edu

The WIDE Research Center investigates how digital technologies—such as the networked personal computer, the Internet and World Wide Web, and computer-based classrooms and workplaces—change the processes, products, and contexts for writing, particularly in organizational and collaborative composing contexts.

Youth Voices

youthvoices.net

Youth Voices is a meeting place where students and their teachers share, distribute, and discuss their inquiries and digital work online to facilitate student-to-student conversations, collaborations, and civic actions that result from publishing and commenting on each other's texts, images, audio, and video.

ACKNOWLEDGMENTS

*B*ecause *Digital Writing Matters,* like its predecessor *Because Writing Matters,* was constructed out of the generosity of the many teacher-consultants and directors in the National Writing Project who shared their stories, their hard work, and their thoughtful questions. We celebrate them as well as Dixie Goswami and our good colleagues in the Bread Loaf Teacher Network, and teachers at the many schools and institutions who also opened up their practice through interviews and site visits. Their commitment to the development of student voices and to inquiry into their own practice puts them on the cutting edge of teaching and learning.

We would also like to acknowledge the work of those educators who took up national and local leadership roles in the various NWP technology projects, from the original e-Design Team to the NWP's Technology Liaisons Network (TLN) and the NWP's Technology Initiative. In particular, we would like to acknowledge Betty Collum, University of Mississippi Writing Project teacher-consultant—a friend, colleague, and TLN Leadership Team member who shared her work for this book but passed away before it could be published.

The work of these leadership teams was strengthened through the support and guidance of NWP leadership, including Executive Director Sharon J. Washington, former Executive Director Richard Sterling, Deputy Director Judy Buchanan, and former and current Associate Directors Marci Resnick, Tanya Baker, and Joye Alberts, along with Program Associate and E-Anthology Coordinator Shirley Brown. Key to bringing teachers' work, questions, and ideas to the surface nationally were Senior Program Associates Christina Cantrill and Paul Oh.

The NWP's Technology Initiative and related Digital Is project work have benefitted from the support of the U.S. Department of Education, in addition to grants from the John D. and Catherine T. MacArthur Foundation's Digital Media and Learning Initiative. We have also benefitted from the insight and support of our thinking partners at Inverness Research Inc. and at our home institutions, Michigan State University and Central Michigan University. And we are grateful to our families for their affirmation and support.

Finally, many hands brought this book into being. Kate Leuschke provided support as the program specialist of the NWP's Digital Is project, and Christina Cantrill, in her role co-directing the Technology Initiative and the Digital Is project, was a central member of the *Because Digital Writing Matters* team, reading and responding to drafts and providing careful feedback. Roxanne Barber and Judith Bess of the NWP's Communications Unit provided excellent editorial support and guidance.

Given the extraordinary work of all these individuals, any errors are the responsibility of the authors.

INDEX